BLACK HISTORY
HISTORY
IN ITS
OWN WORDS

IMAGE COMICS, INC.
Robert Kirkman — Chief Operating Officer
Erik Larsen — Chief Financial Officer
Todd McFarlane — President
Marc Silvestri — Chief Executive Officer
Jim Valentino — Vice-President

Eric Stephenson — Publisher
Corey Murphy — Director of Sales
Jeff Boison — Director of Publishing Planning & Book Trade Sales
Chris Ross — Director of Digital Sales
Kat Salazar — Director of PR & Marketing
Branwyn Bigglestone — Controller
Drew Gill — Art Director
Brett Warnock — Production Manager
Meredith Wallace — Print Manager
Briah Skelly — Publicist
Aly Hoffman — Conventions & Events Coordinator
Sasha Head — Sales & Marketing Production Designer
David Brothers — Branding Manager
Melissa Gifford — Content Manager
Erika Schnatz — Production Artist
Ryan Brewer — Production Artist
Shanna Matuszak — Production Artist
Tricia Ramos — Production Artist
Vincent Kukua — Production Artist
Jeff Stang — Direct Market Sales Representative
Emilio Bautista — Digital Sales Associate
Leanna Caunter — Accounting Assistant
Chloe Ramos-Peterson — Library Market Sales Representative
IMAGECOMICS.COM

BLACK HISTORY IN ITS OWN WORDS
February 2017. First Printing.
ISBN: 978-1-5343-0153-5

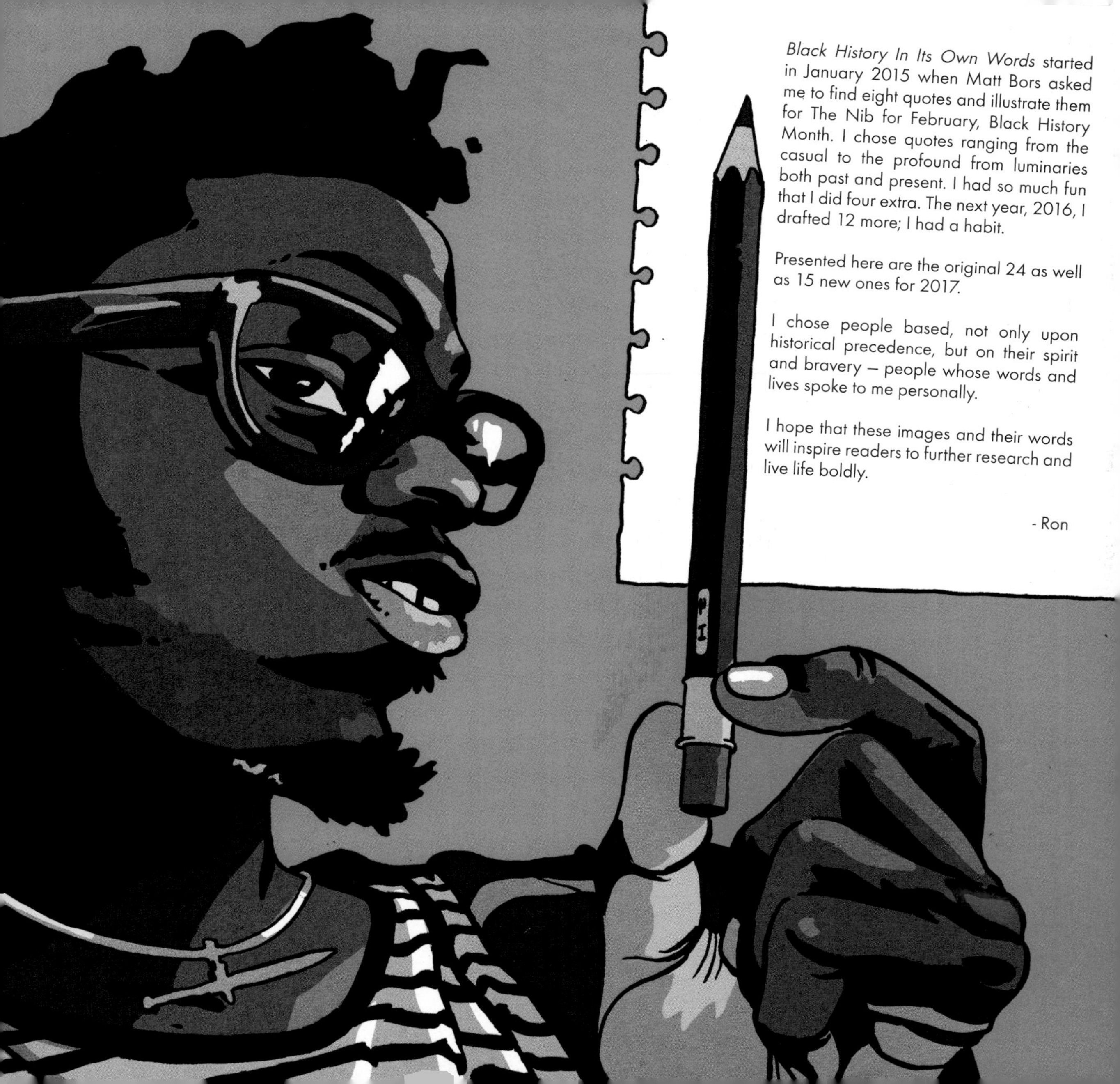

Black History In Its Own Words started in January 2015 when Matt Bors asked me to find eight quotes and illustrate them for The Nib for February, Black History Month. I chose quotes ranging from the casual to the profound from luminaries both past and present. I had so much fun that I did four extra. The next year, 2016, I drafted 12 more; I had a habit.

Presented here are the original 24 as well as 15 new ones for 2017.

I chose people based, not only upon historical precedence, but on their spirit and bravery – people whose words and lives spoke to me personally.

I hope that these images and their words will inspire readers to further research and live life boldly.

- Ron

2015

Angela Yvonne Davis

Angela Davis was part of the vanguard of the 1960s Black Power movement. She has worked with the Black Panther Party and the United States Comunist Party. She continues to fight systemic inequities and is a major force in the prison abolition movement.

Quote from Davis' book *Women, Culture and Politics (1989).*

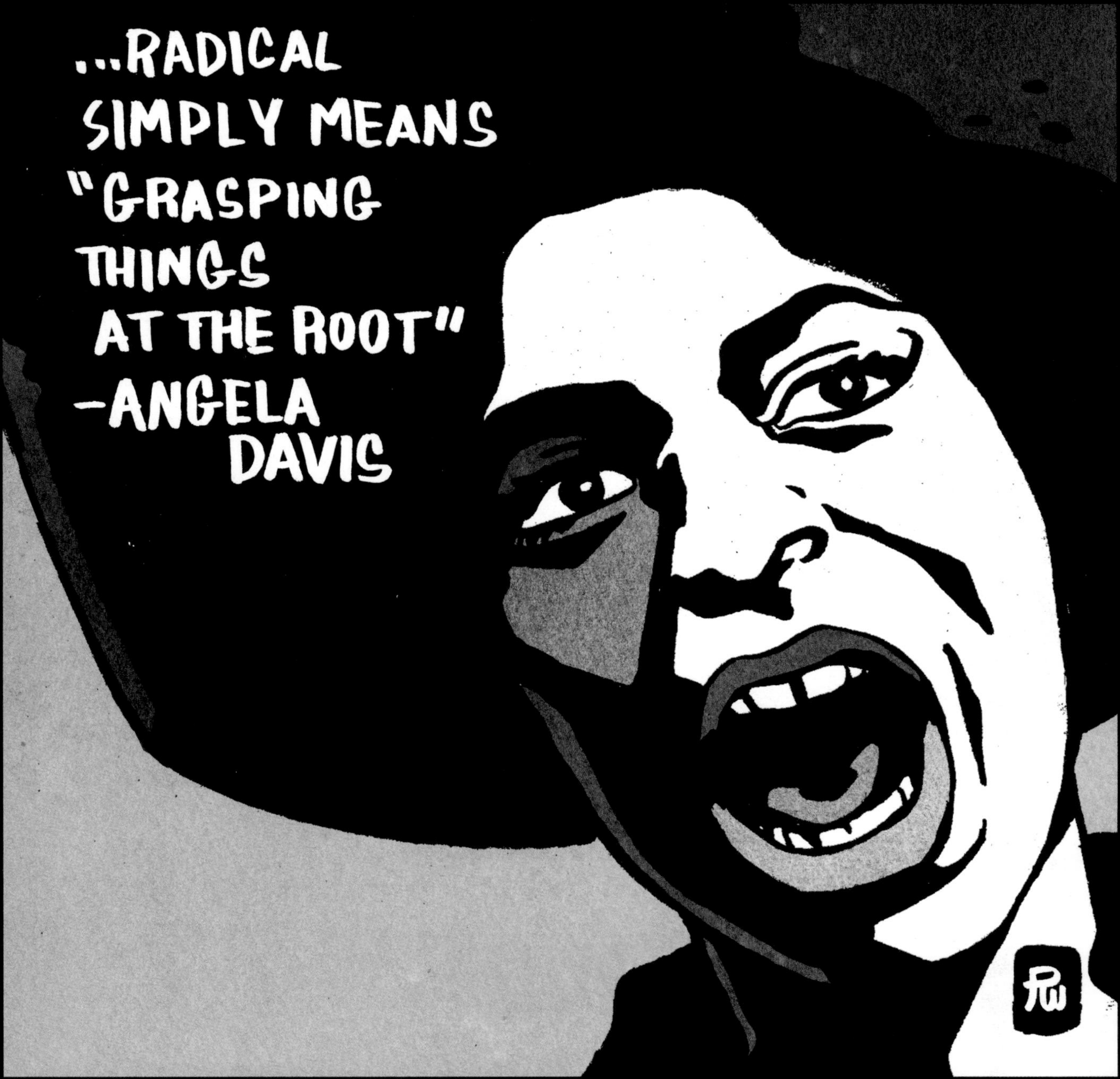
...RADICAL SIMPLY MEANS "GRASPING THINGS AT THE ROOT" -ANGELA DAVIS
PW

MC Ride

MC Ride is the vocalist of Death Grips. Under his given name, Stefan Burnett, he is also an accomplished visual artist.

Quote taken from *Death Grips, Exmilitary "Beware" (2011).*

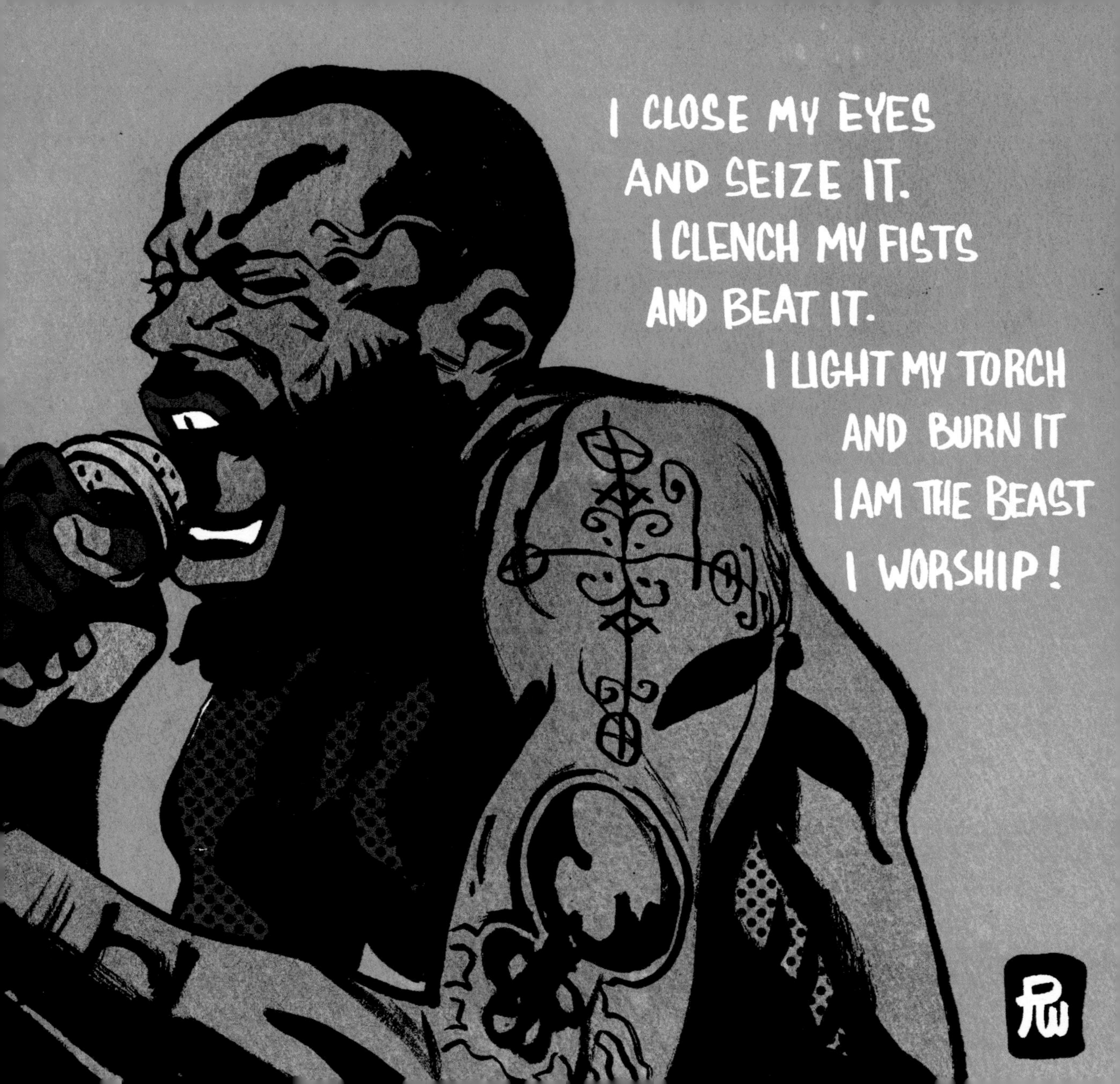
I CLOSE MY EYES
AND SEIZE IT.
I CLENCH MY FISTS
AND BEAT IT.
I LIGHT MY TORCH
AND BURN IT
I AM THE BEAST
I WORSHIP!

George Joseph Herriman

George Herriman is one of the forefathers of American cartooning. His strip *Krazy Kat*, the first cat and mouse cartoon, laid the foundation for many to come and have influenced many great cartoonists.

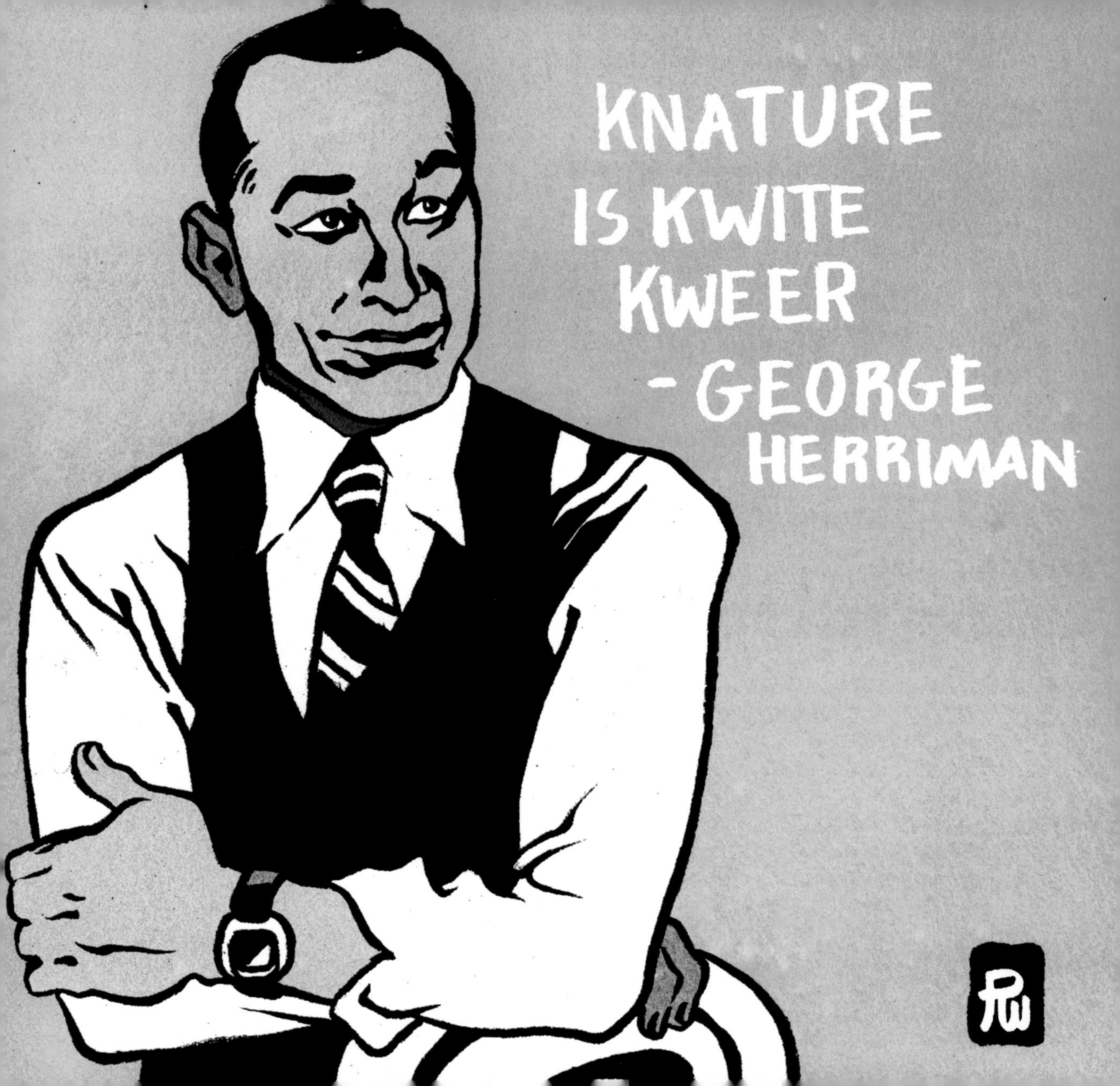
KNATURE IS KWITE KWEER
- GEORGE HERRIMAN
PW

Ice Cube

As a member of the rap collective N.W.A, Ice Cube pioneered the gangster rap genre; his talent as a writer and producer made him a pillar of West Coast rap's formative years.

Cube has also garnered great success in film as an actor and producer.

Quote taken from *Time Magazine, June 2014, "Ten Questions"* with Belinda Luscombe.

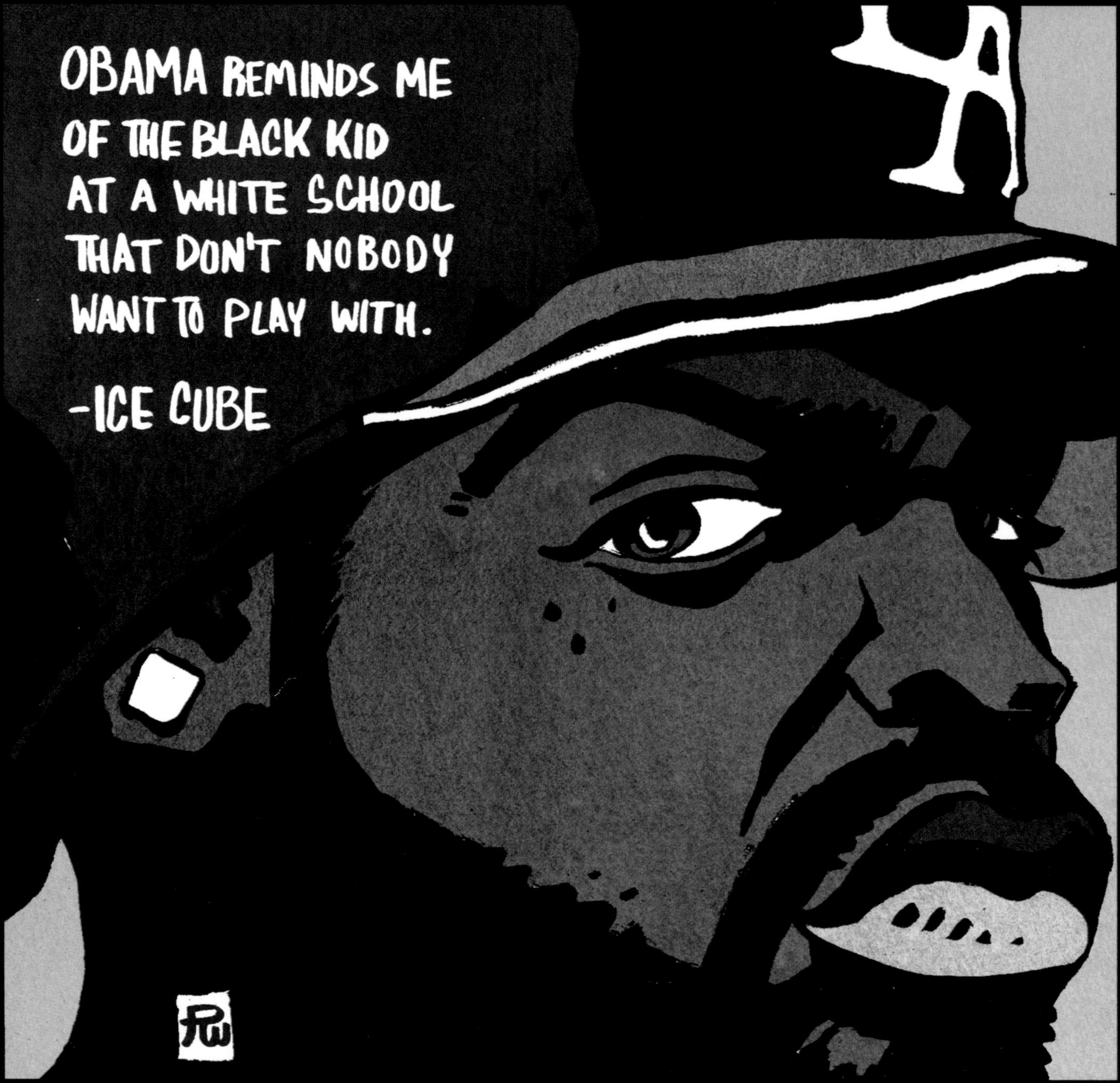
OBAMA REMINDS ME OF THE BLACK KID AT A WHITE SCHOOL THAT DON'T NOBODY WANT TO PLAY WITH.
-ICE CUBE
PW

Saul Williams

Poet, actor, musician, Saul Williams came to prominence in the 1990s Slam Poetry scene, seamlessly bridging the disciplines of hip-hop, spoken word, and radical progressive intellectualism. His genre fluidity defies definition.

This quote came out in private conversation. Though he said I said it, I'm pretty sure he said it first.

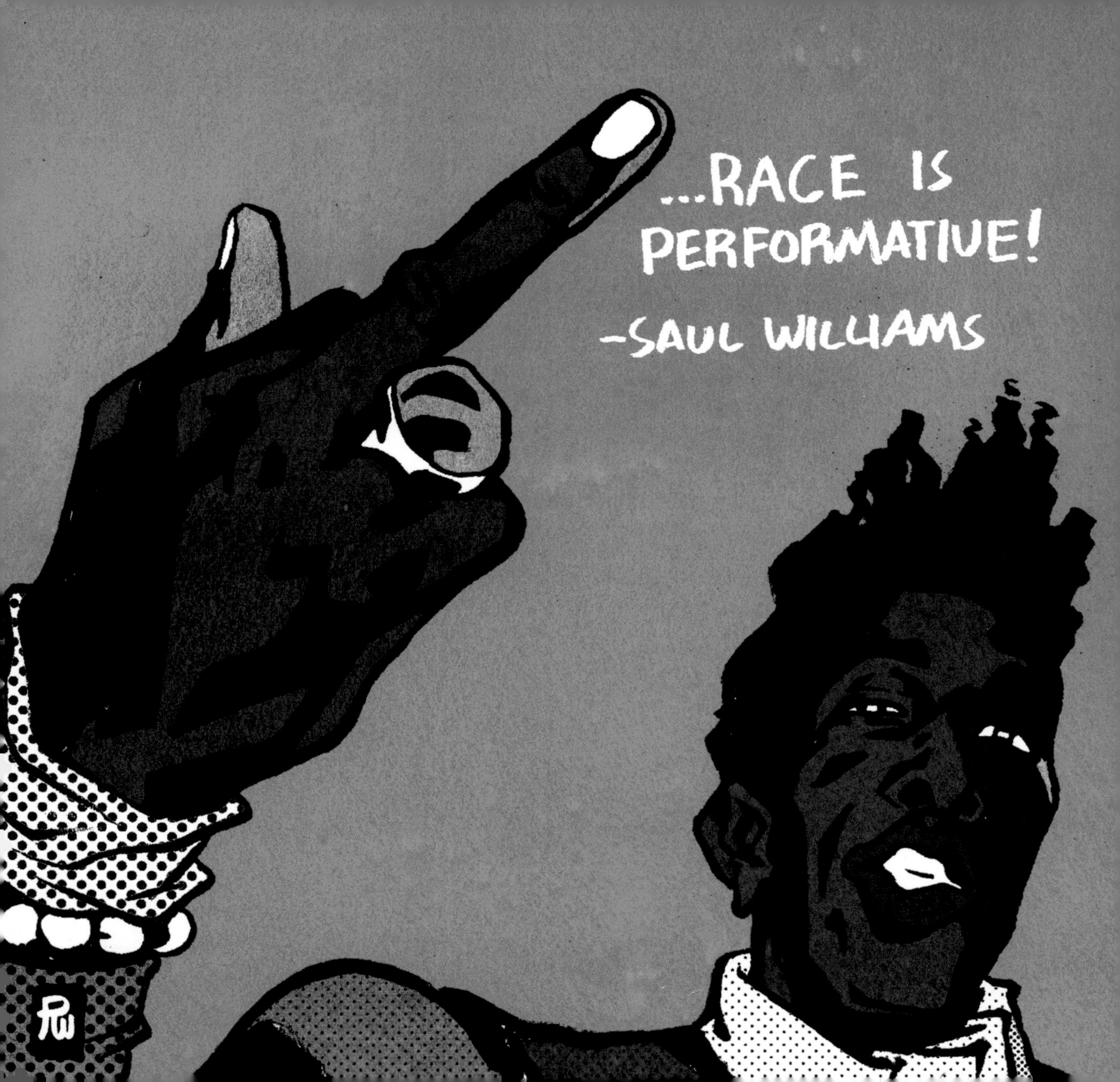
...RACE IS PERFORMATIVE!
-SAUL WILLIAMS
PW

Dave Chappelle

Dave Chappelle's comedy casually cuts to the core of the human condition and contemporary society in the tradition of performers like Dick Gregory and Richard Pryor.

This quote is taken from *James Lipton's Inside the Actors Studio (2006)*.

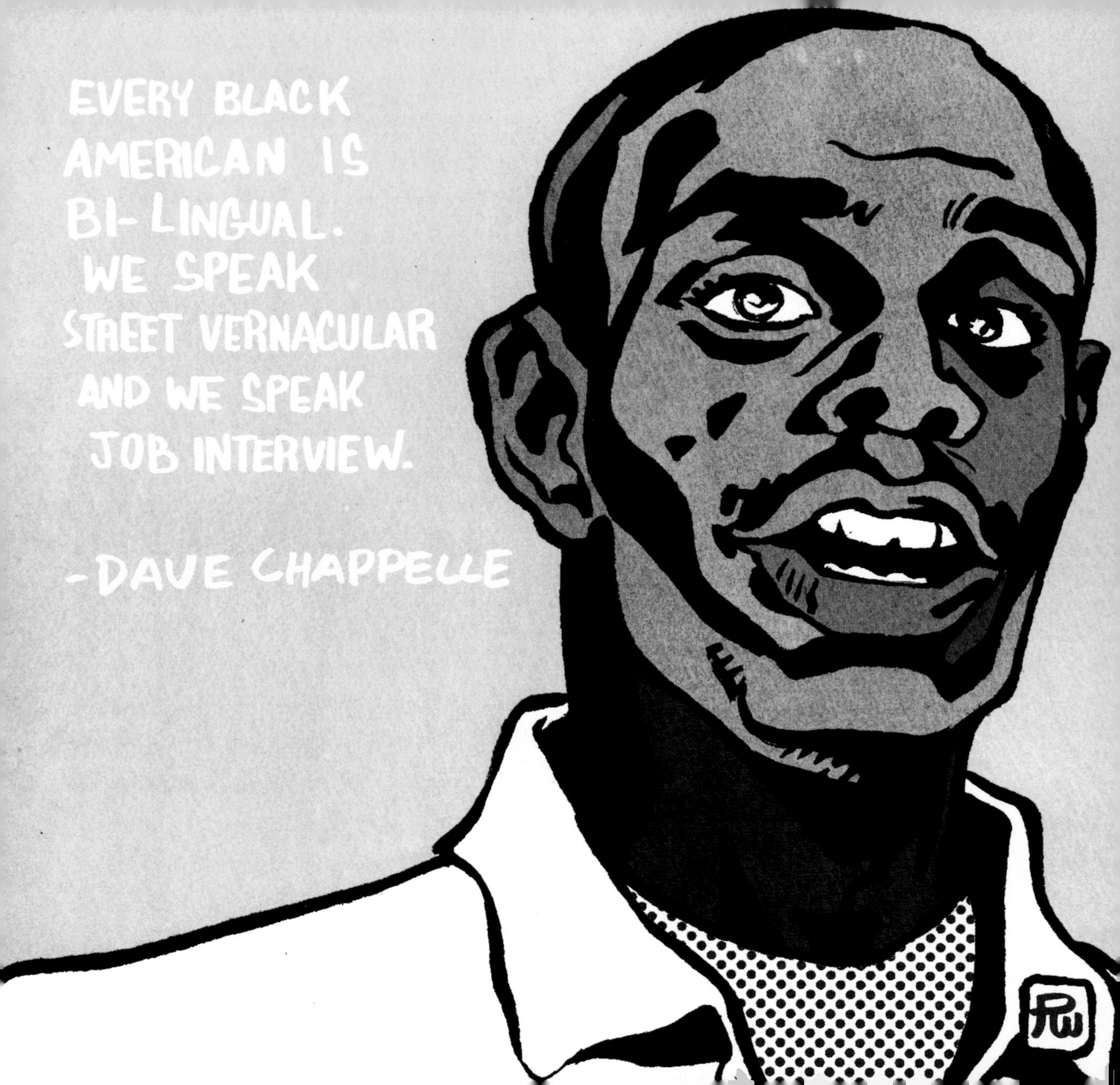
EVERY BLACK AMERICAN IS BI-LINGUAL. WE SPEAK STREET VERNACULAR AND WE SPEAK JOB INTERVIEW.
-DAVE CHAPPELLE
PW

Spike Lee

Cinema auteur, Spike Lee sparked a new wave of '90s cinema that trained a lens on the complexities of black American life. His work as filmmaker, producer, and businessman remains a powerful force in visual culture.

Quote taken from a lecture at Pratt Institute in February 2014.

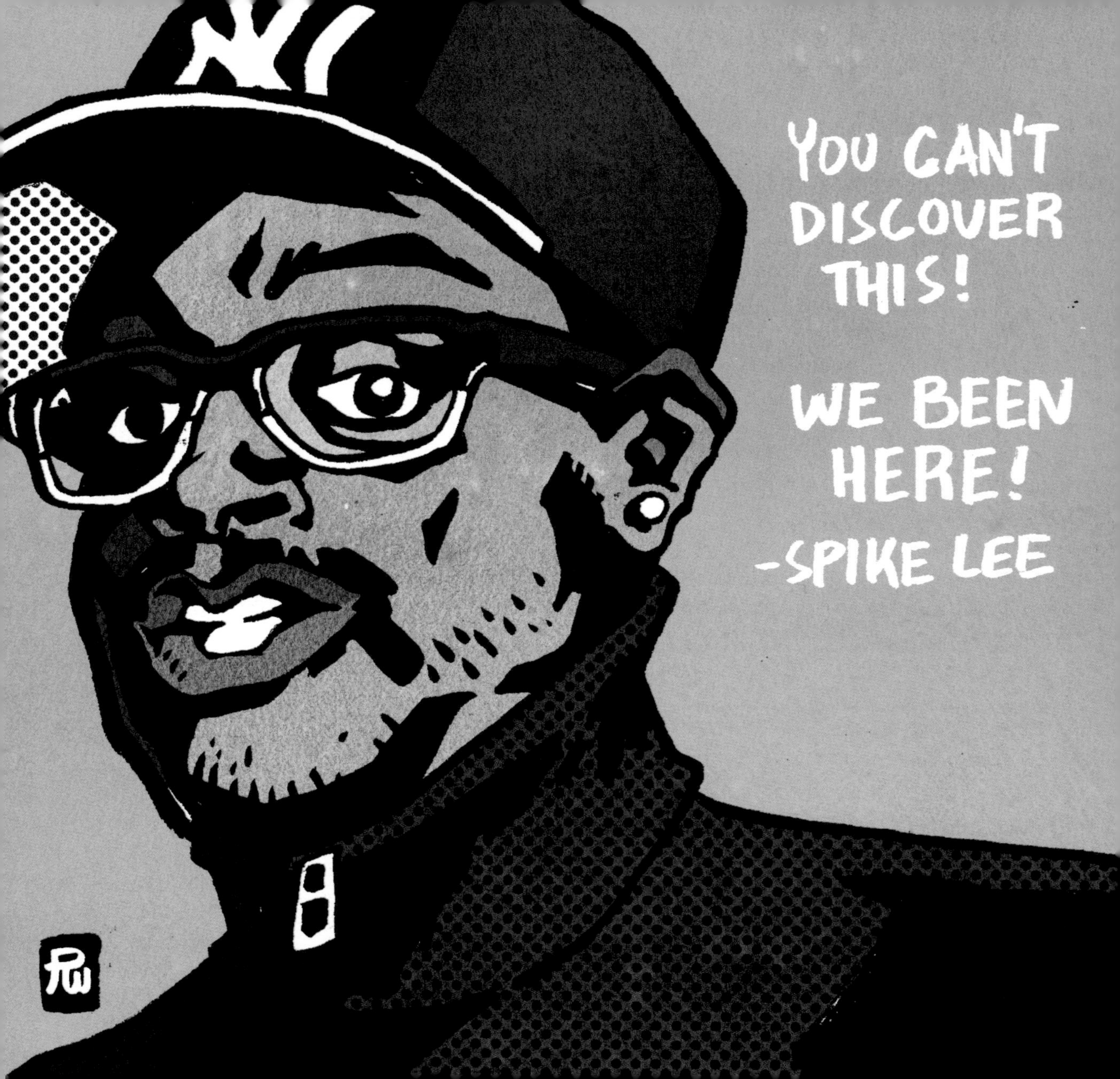
YOU CAN'T DISCOVER THIS!
WE BEEN HERE!
-SPIKE LEE

Arturo Alfonso Schomburg

Archivist and activist Arturo Schomburg figured prominently in the Harlem Renaissance. His work and collection laid the foundation for the Schomburg Center for Research in Black Culture in Harlem.

Quote taken from the essay *"The Negro Digs Up His Past"* *(1925)*.

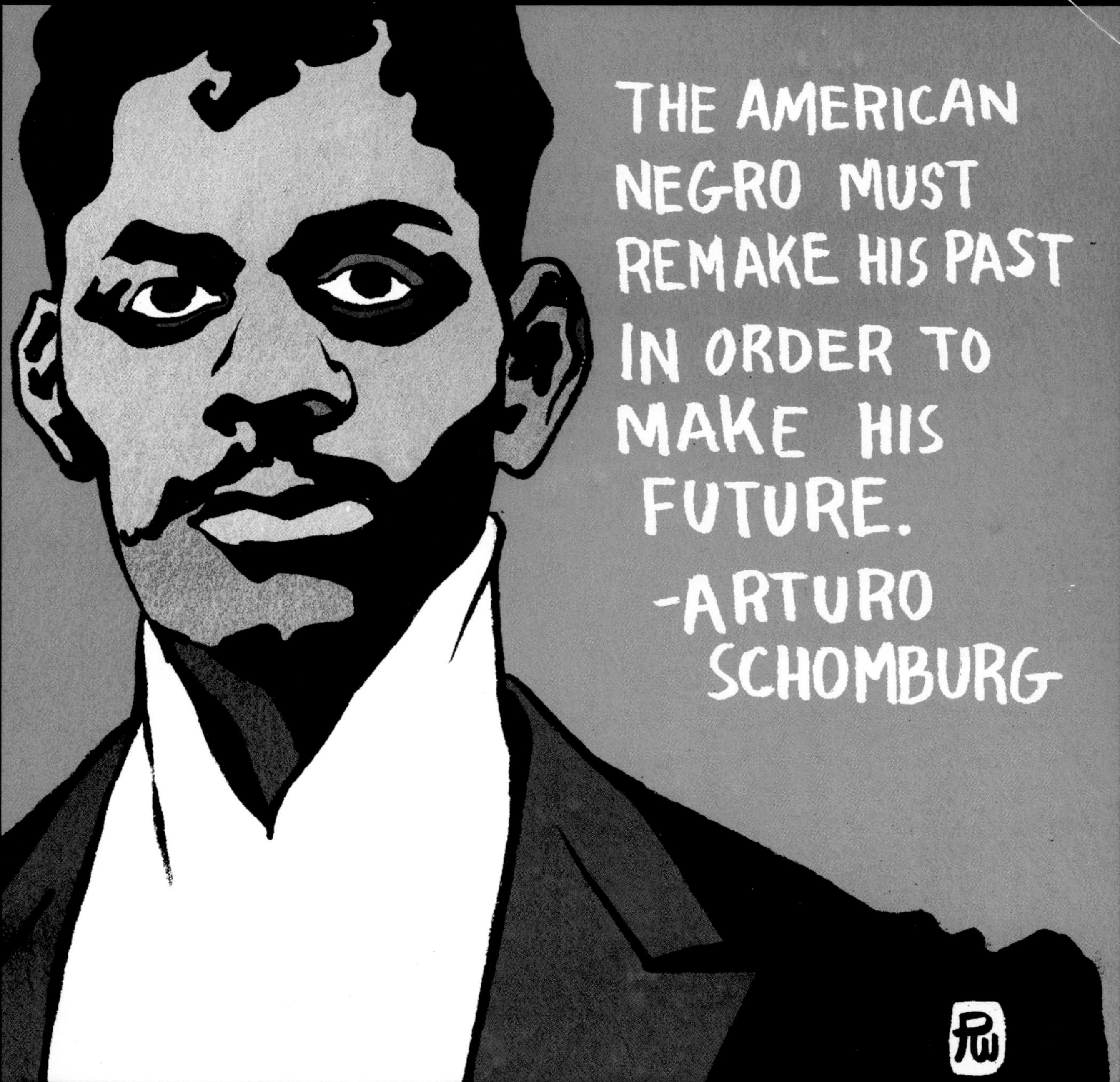
THE AMERICAN NEGRO MUST REMAKE HIS PAST IN ORDER TO MAKE HIS FUTURE.
-ARTURO SCHOMBURG
PW

Laverne Cox

Laverne Cox is a performer and producer. She is an outspoken advocate for LGBTQ rights and gender equality.

Quote taken from *The Daily Beast* article *"Laverne Cox Talks Love, Healing, and Pride"* (June 14, 2016).

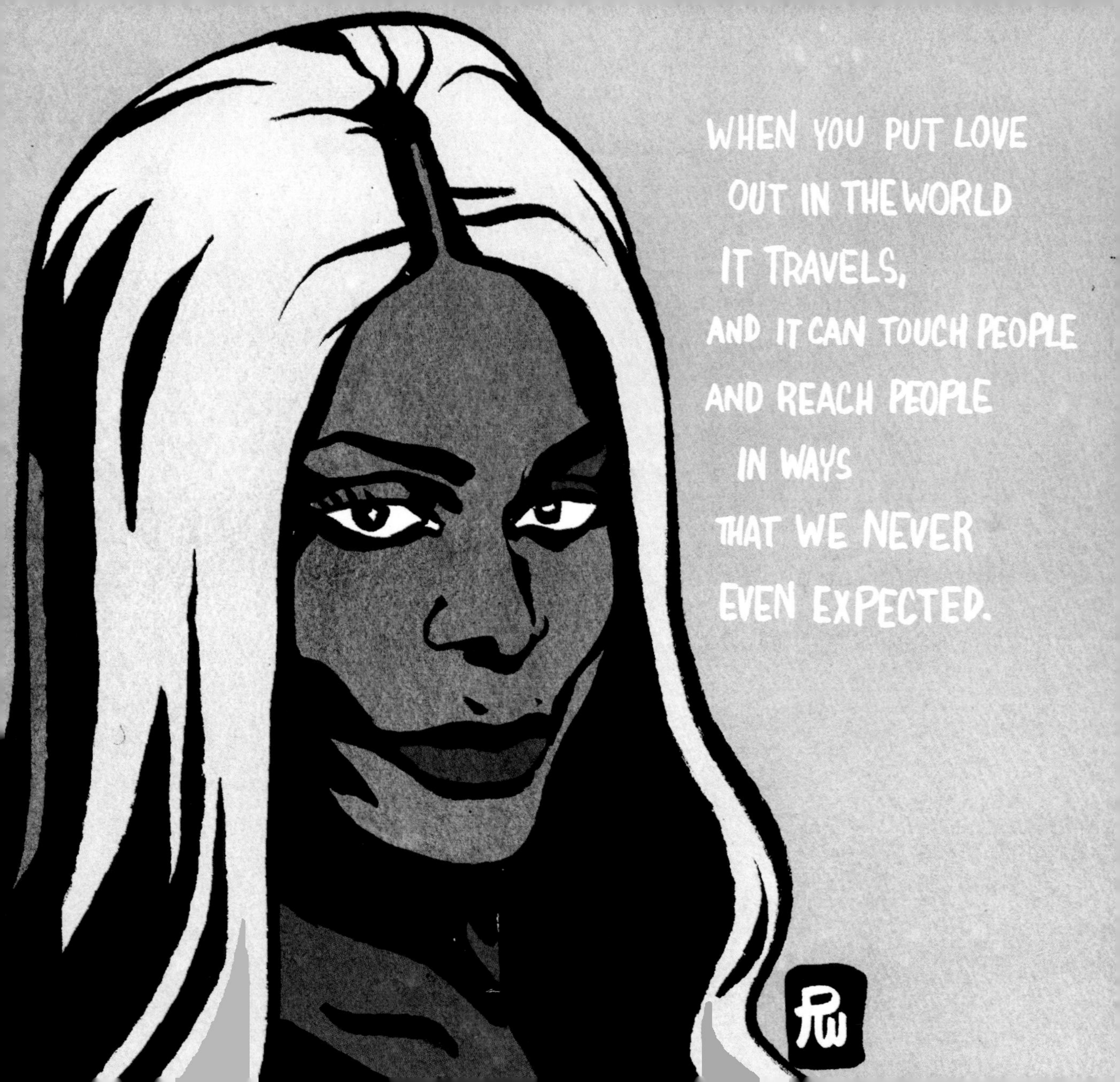
WHEN YOU PUT LOVE
OUT IN THE WORLD
IT TRAVELS,
AND IT CAN TOUCH PEOPLE
AND REACH PEOPLE
IN WAYS
THAT WE NEVER
EVEN EXPECTED.

James Baldwin

An accomplished essayist, author, and orator, James Baldwin deconstructed race, sex, and economics in public debate and in narrative.

Quote taken from an article in the *1962 Negro Digest, "The Negro's Role in American Culture."*

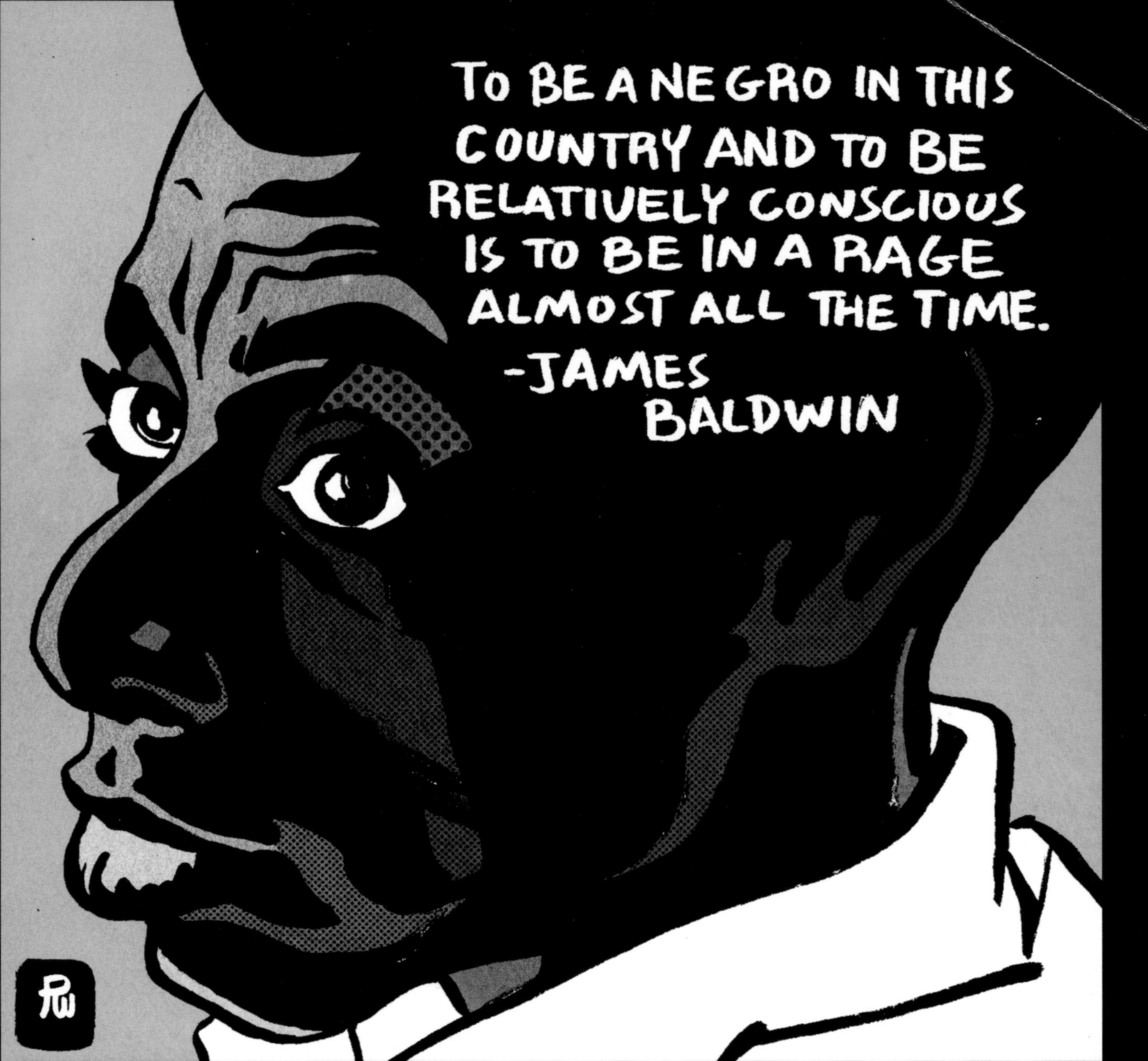
TO BE A NEGRO IN THIS COUNTRY AND TO BE RELATIVELY CONSCIOUS IS TO BE IN A RAGE ALMOST ALL THE TIME.
-JAMES BALDWIN
PW

Audre Lorde

Audre Lorde's work as a poet, essayist, and activist set the table for critical dialogue on the intesection of race, sex, and structural inequity and how those dialogues, independent of each other, are incomplete.

Quote taken from the title of Lorde's essay *"The Master's Tools Will Never Dismantle the Master's House,"* printed in *Sister Outsider: Essays and Speeches (1984).*

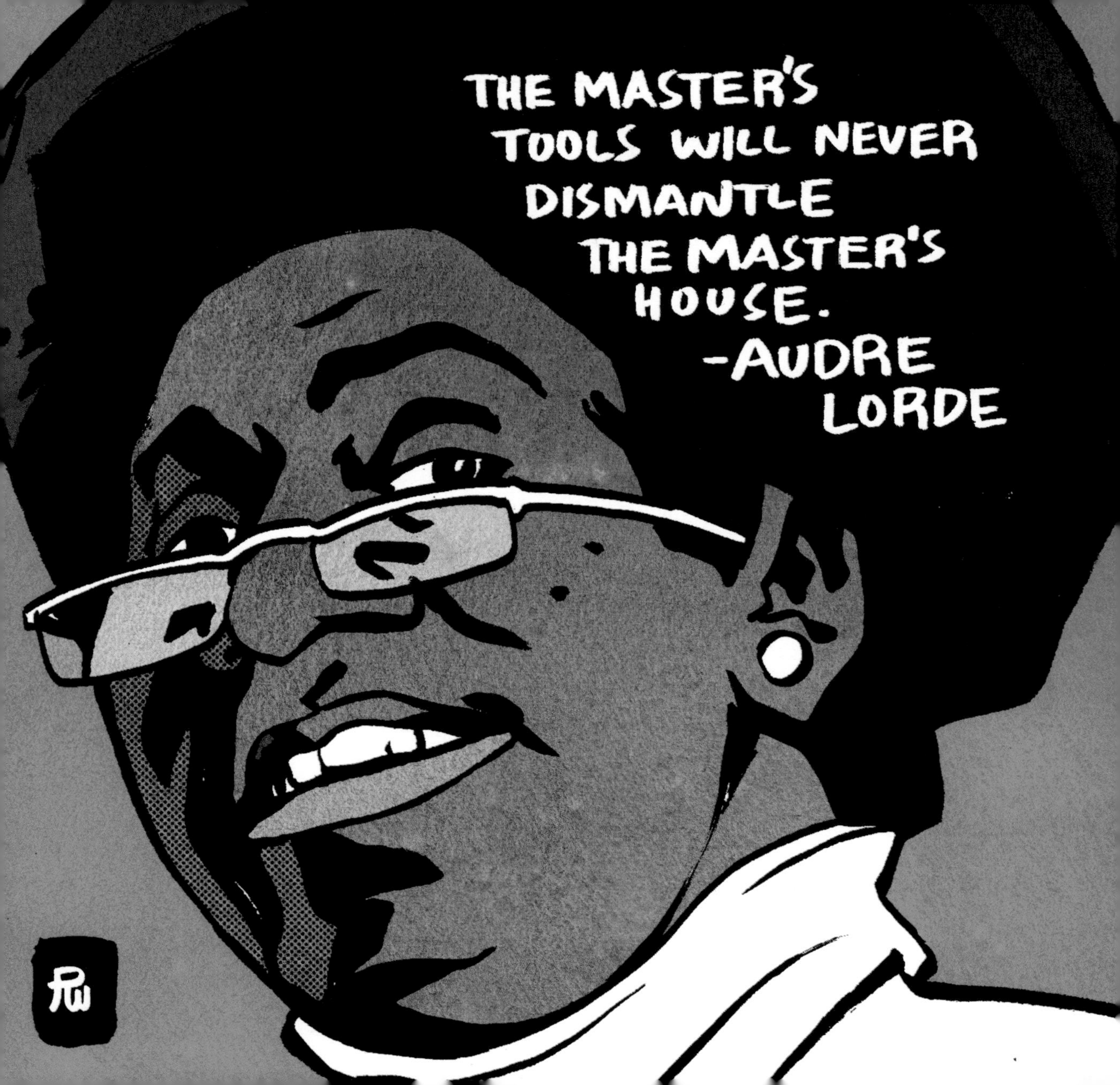
THE MASTER'S TOOLS WILL NEVER DISMANTLE THE MASTER'S HOUSE.
-AUDRE LORDE
PW

Lena Horne

Lena Horne sacrificed her Hollywood career to call attention to civil rights and economic injustice. Despite being blacklisted by Hollywood, Horne remained a force of art, culture, and activism.

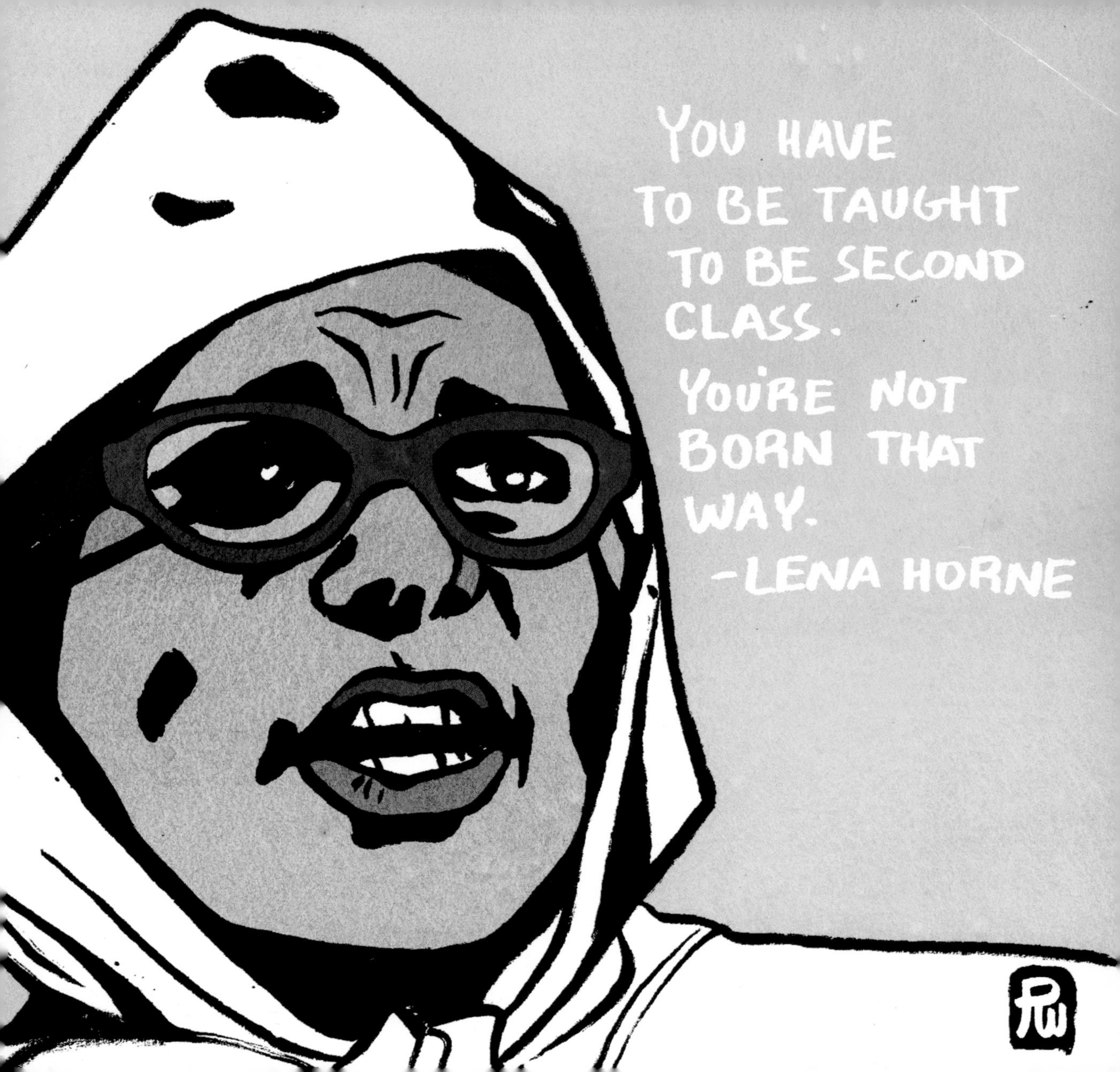
YOU HAVE
TO BE TAUGHT
TO BE SECOND
CLASS.
YOU'RE NOT
BORN THAT
WAY.
-LENA HORNE

2016

Kimberly Bryant

After a successful career as an electrical engineer, Kimberly Bryant started *Black Girls Code* to teach black school-age girls in underserved communities how to code.

Quote taken from an interview on *whitehouse.gov*, *"Connecting Kids from Diverse Backgrounds to Tech Skills."*

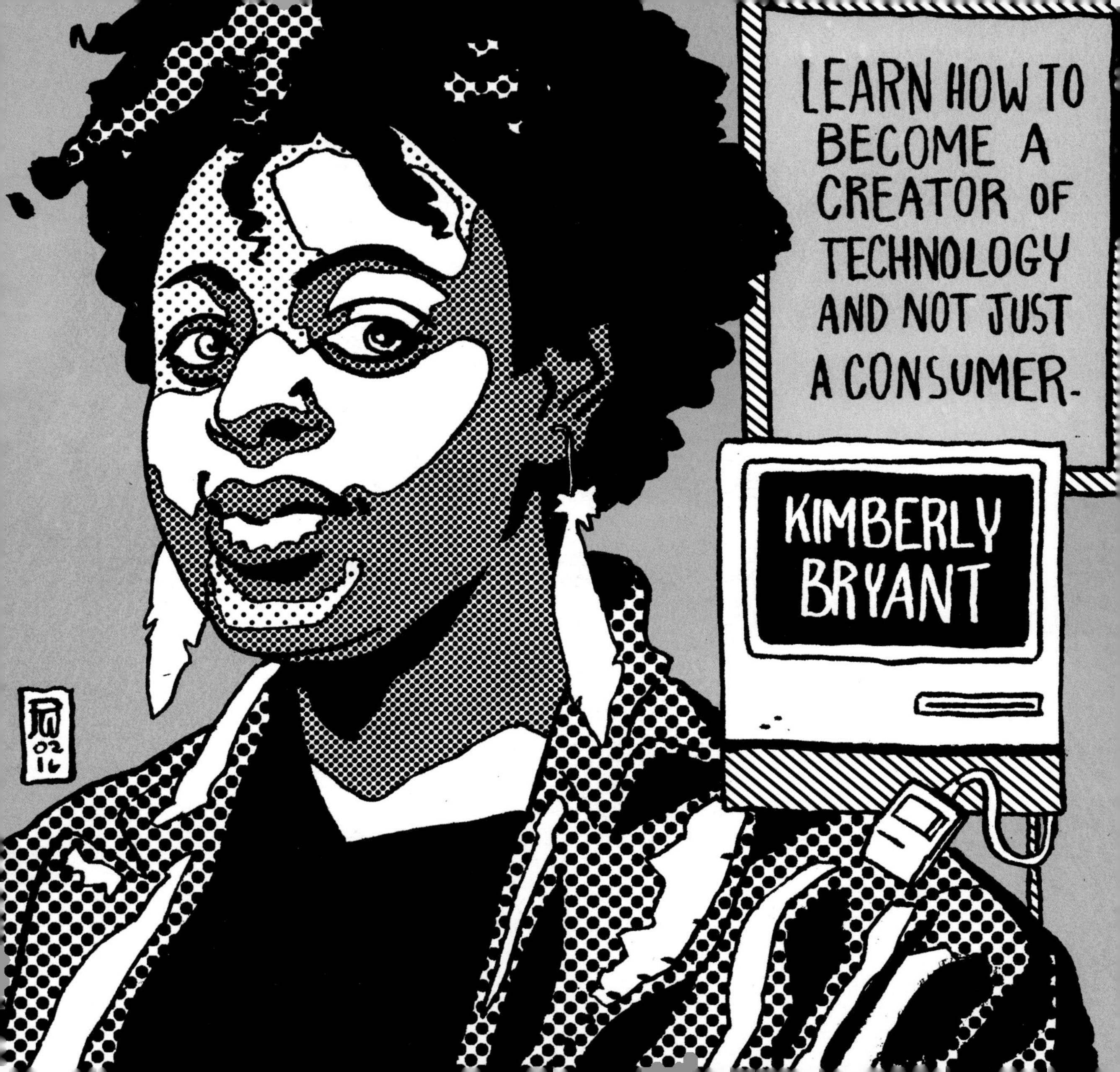
LEARN HOW TO BECOME A CREATOR OF TECHNOLOGY AND NOT JUST A CONSUMER.
KIMBERLY BRYANT
RW 02 16

Fred Hampton

As deputy chairman of the Black Panther Party, Fred Hampton reached out to all communities, even poor, rural white communities, to unify and oppose the economic exploitation of the poor and working class.

He was assassinated in his sleep by the United Stated Government.

Quote taken from an excerpt of a speech given shortly before his death, replayed in the documentary *The Murder of Fred Hampton (1971)*.

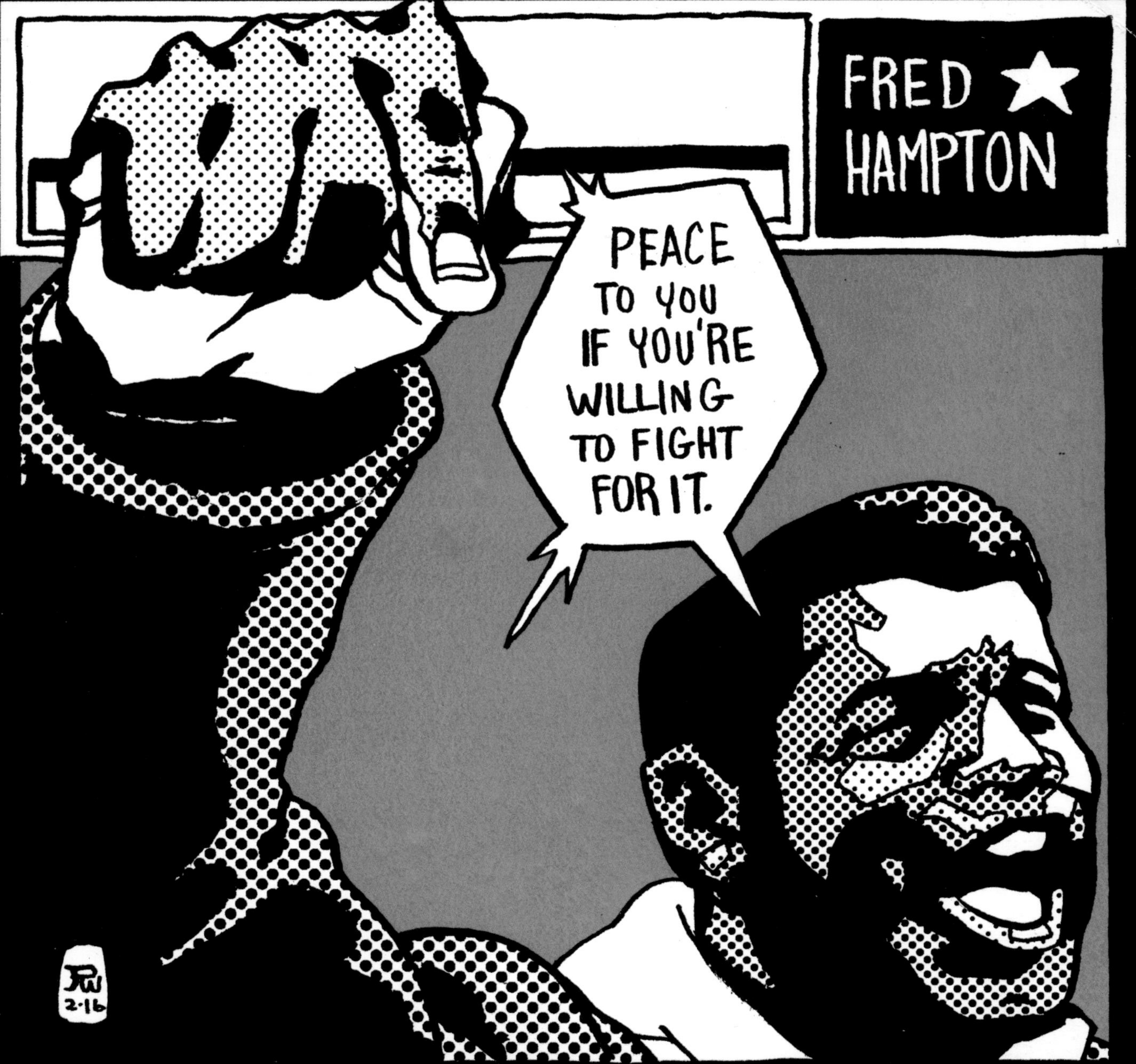
FRED ★ HAMPTON
PEACE TO YOU IF YOU'RE WILLING TO FIGHT FOR IT.
2-16

Serena Williams

Serena Williams is one of the most accomplished athletes of all time. Her combination of power and grace has set a new precedent in tennis. The Women's Tennis Association has ranked Williams number one on six separate occasions. She holds the most major titles of any kind in tennis, male or female.

She is unequaled.

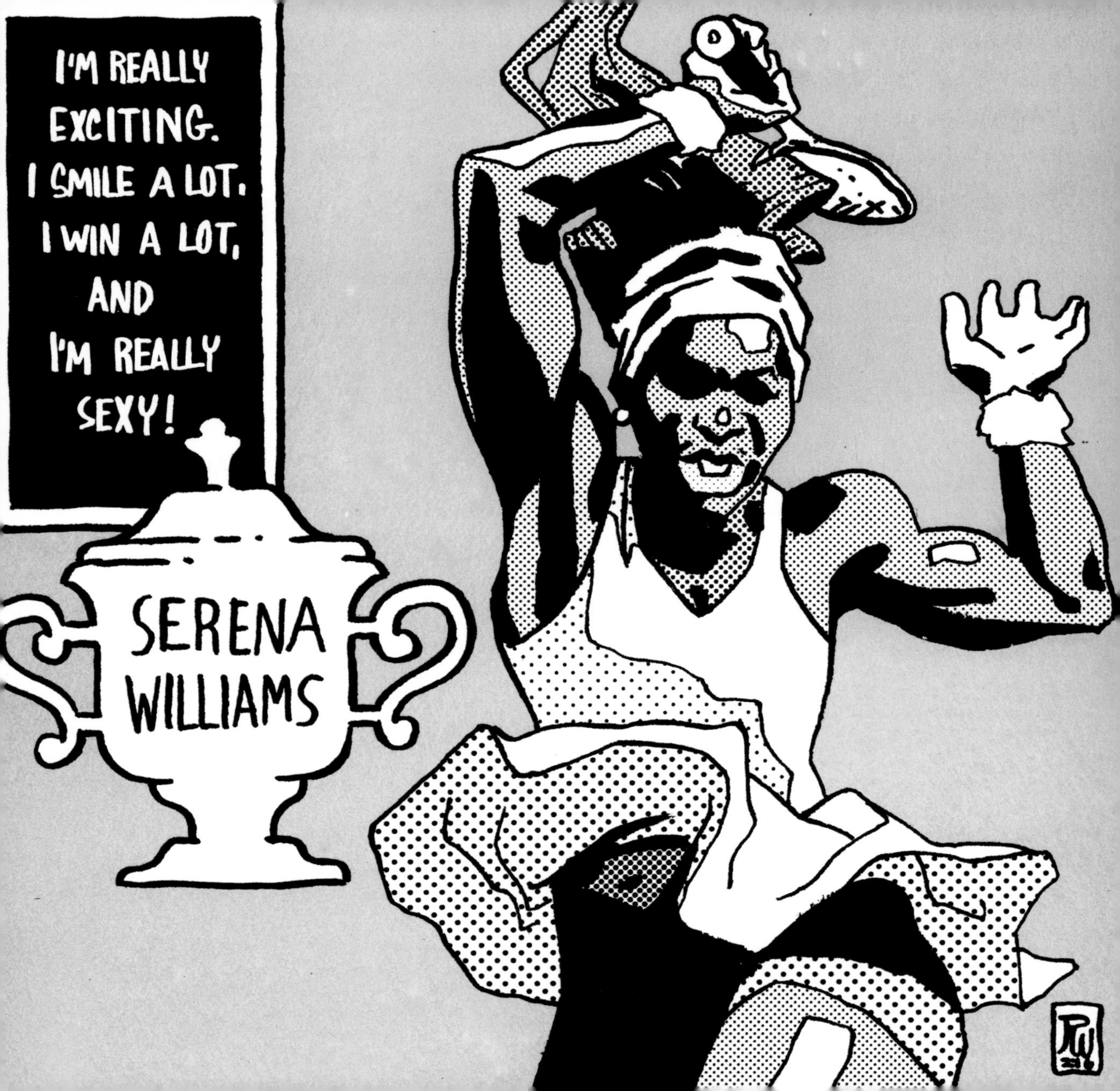
I'M REALLY EXCITING.
I SMILE A LOT.
I WIN A LOT,
AND
I'M REALLY SEXY!
SERENA WILLIAMS

Poly Styrene

Poly Styrene was a vanguard of the 1970s UK punk scene as frontwoman of the band X-Ray Spex. She was unique, even among punks. Her vocal style set a standard and her visual style set her apart.

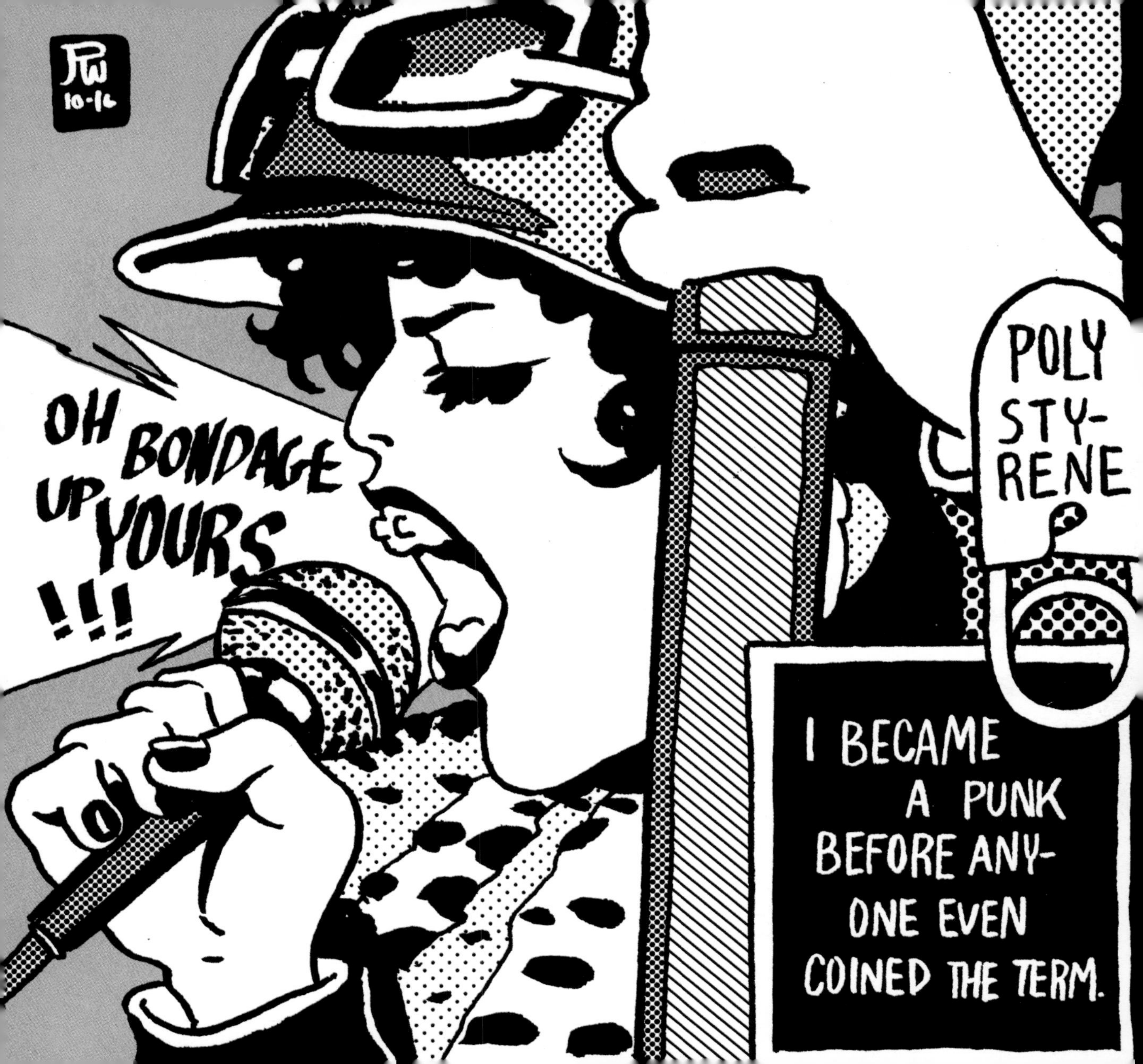
PW 10-16
OH BONDAGE UP YOURS!!!
POLY STY- RENE
I BECAME A PUNK BEFORE ANY- ONE EVEN COINED THE TERM.

Mykki Blanco

As part of the avant garde of rap counterculture. Mykki Blanco smashes conventional modes of thinking regarding art, sex, and gender.

Quote taken from 2012 Pitchfork article *"We Invented Swag: NYC's Queer Rap."*

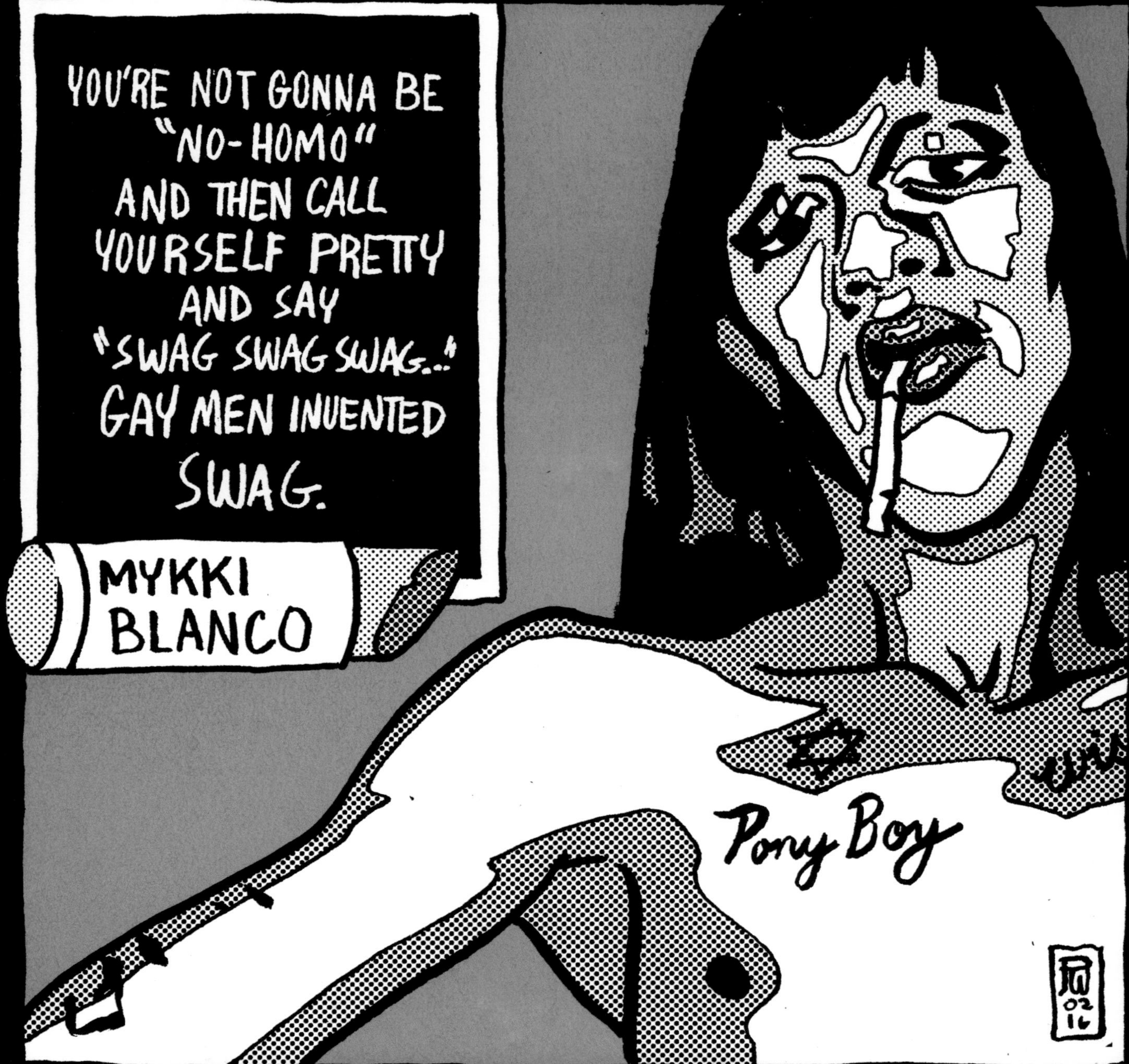
YOU'RE NOT GONNA BE "NO-HOMO" AND THEN CALL YOURSELF PRETTY AND SAY "SWAG SWAG SWAG..." GAY MEN INVENTED SWAG.
MYKKI BLANCO
Pony Boy

Octavia Butler

Octavia Butler is a pioneer in speculative fiction. Her work is marked in its inclusion of and focusing on people of the African diaspora, particularly women, as well as its exploration of the human body and its relation to identity.

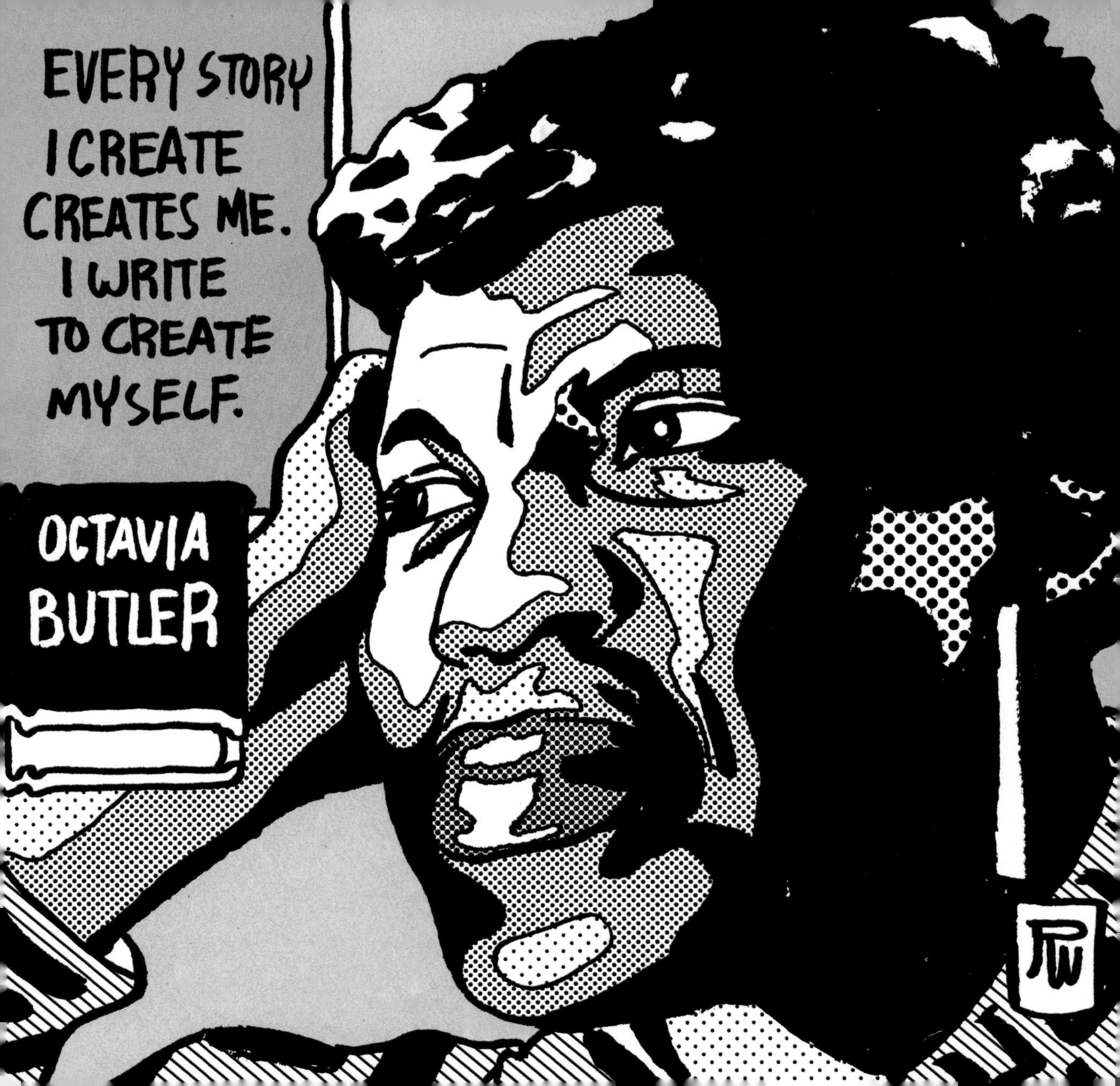
EVERY STORY I CREATE CREATES ME. I WRITE TO CREATE MYSELF.
OCTAVIA BUTLER
PW

Zadie Smith

Zadie Smith explores the nuance, minutae, and seeming contradictions of life through her novels and essays.

Quote from her first novel, *White Teeth (2000)*.

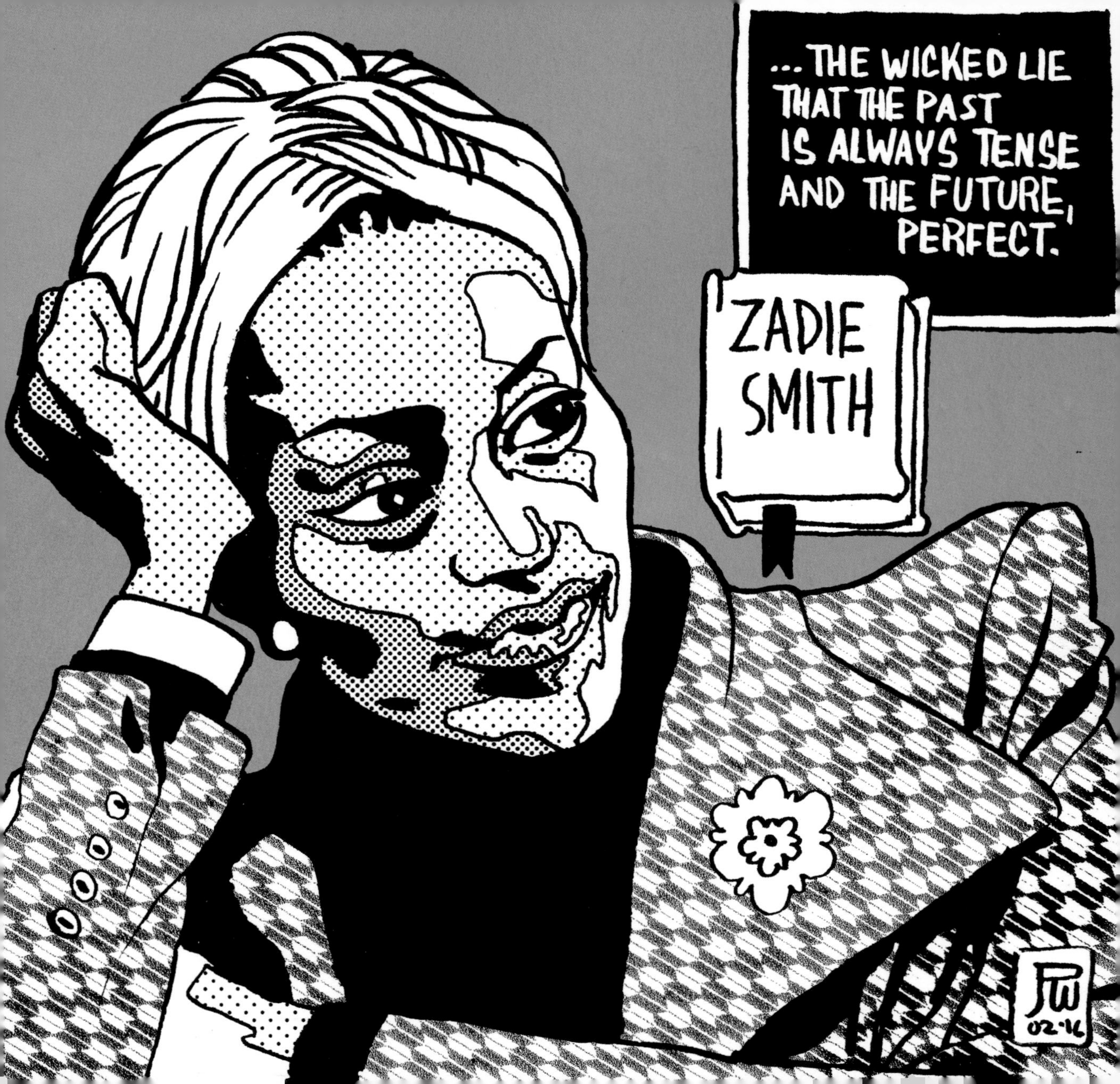
...THE WICKED LIE THAT THE PAST IS ALWAYS TENSE AND THE FUTURE, PERFECT.
ZADIE SMITH
PW 02-16

Kanye West

Kanye West is a highly visible pop artist and music producer who uses fame as a medium and a platform to pursue design. His creative efforts have pushed the boundaries of the expression of black male identity.

Quote taken from his feature on A$AP Rocky's *"Jukebox Joints"* *(2015).*

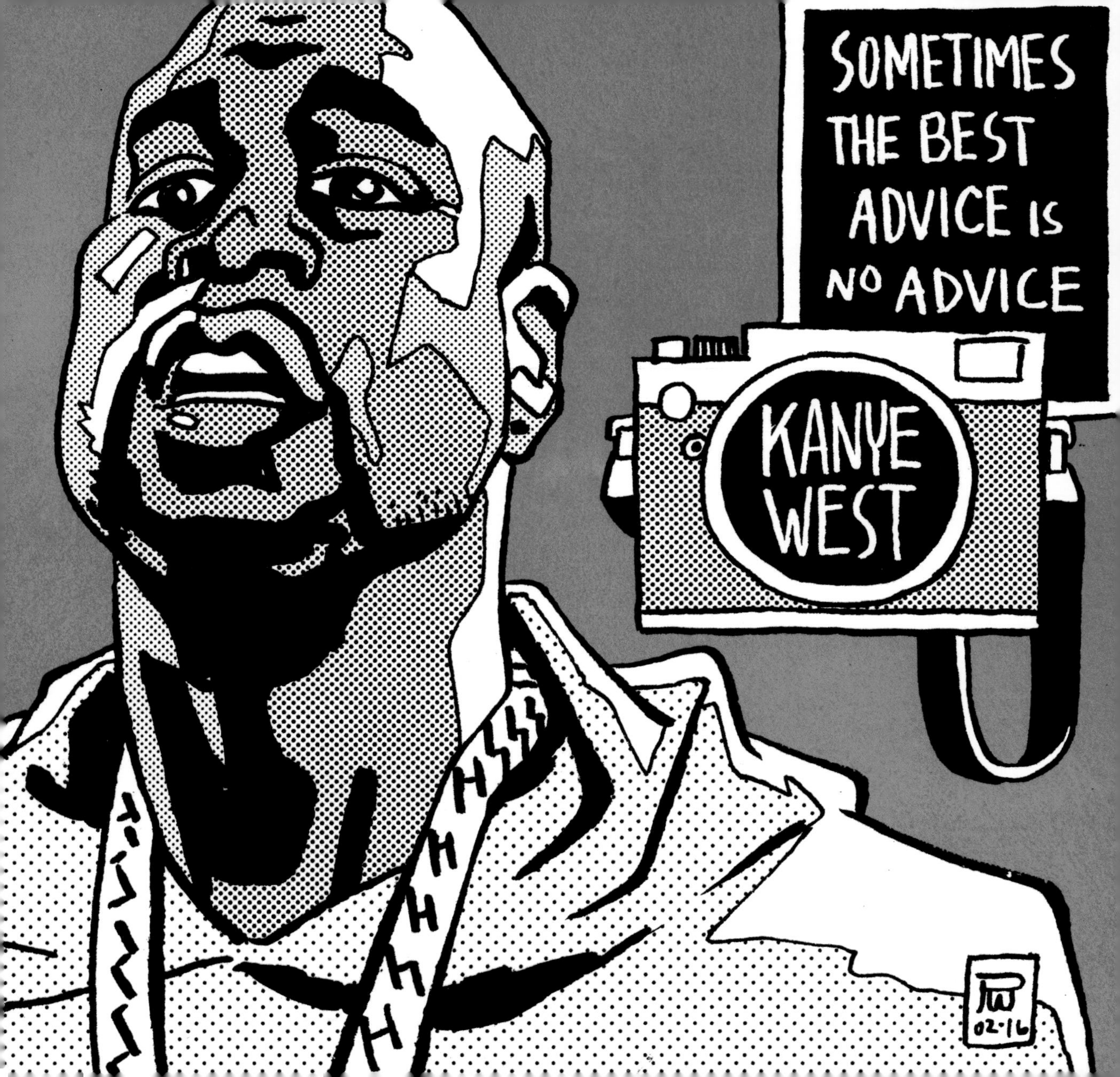
SOMETIMES THE BEST ADVICE IS NO ADVICE
KANYE WEST

Shirley Chisholm

A fierce intellectual, Shirley Chisholm took her seat as the first black woman elected to Congress in 1968 and in 1972 was the first woman to run for the presidential nomination of the Democratic Party. Chisholm boldly advocated for the integration of people of all types into the United States Democratic process.

Quote taken from Chisholm's 1970 book, *Unbought and Unbossed*.

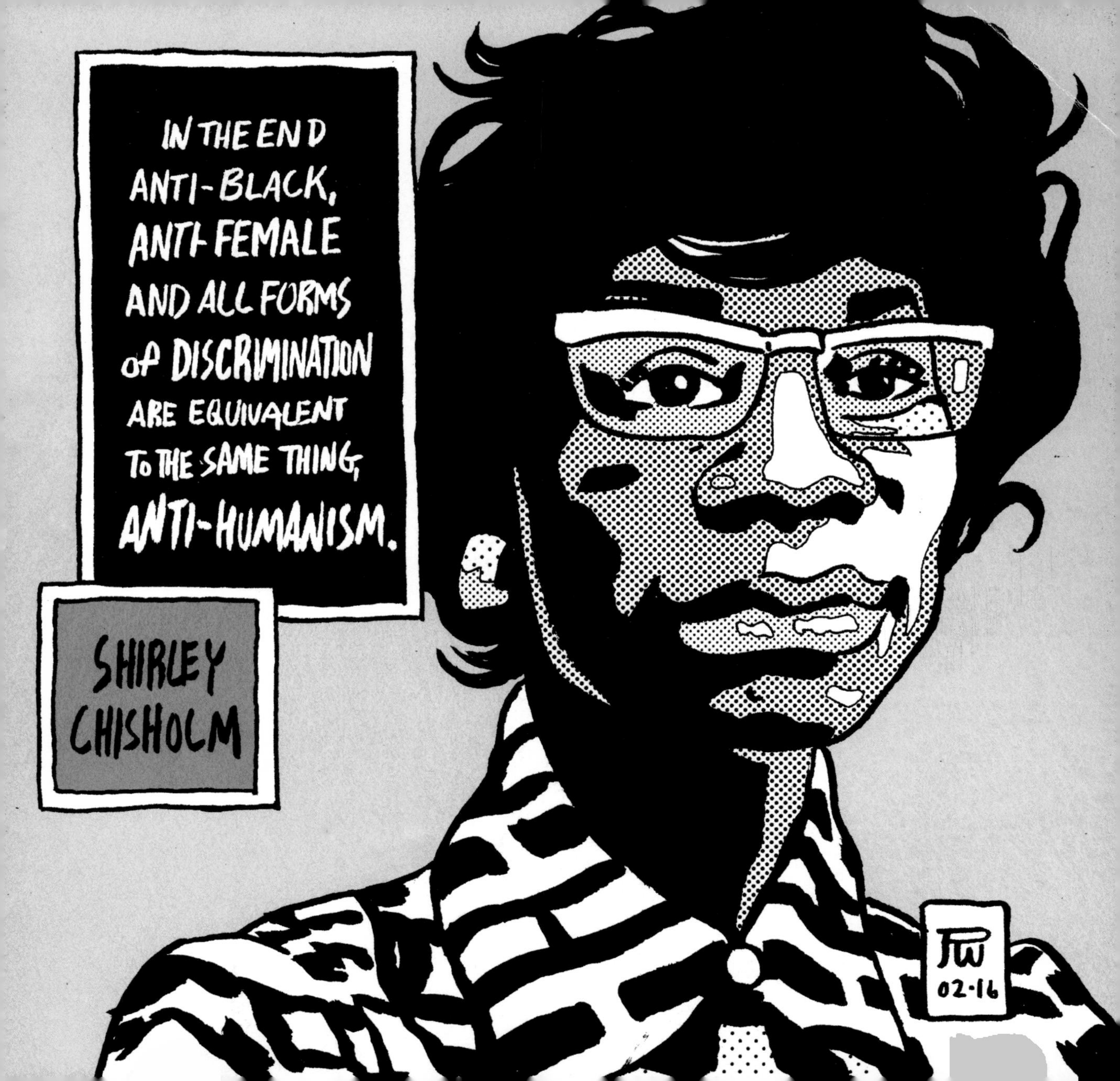
IN THE END ANTI-BLACK, ANTI-FEMALE AND ALL FORMS OF DISCRIMINATION ARE EQUIVALENT TO THE SAME THING, ANTI-HUMANISM.
SHIRLEY CHISHOLM
JW
02-16

Jean-Michel Basquiat

Jean-Michel Basquiat merged sophisticated semiotics with playful language, samples, and appropriations to create work that both embodied the counterculture and economic explosion of '80s New York and the entirety of the complex relationship between Africa and the western world.

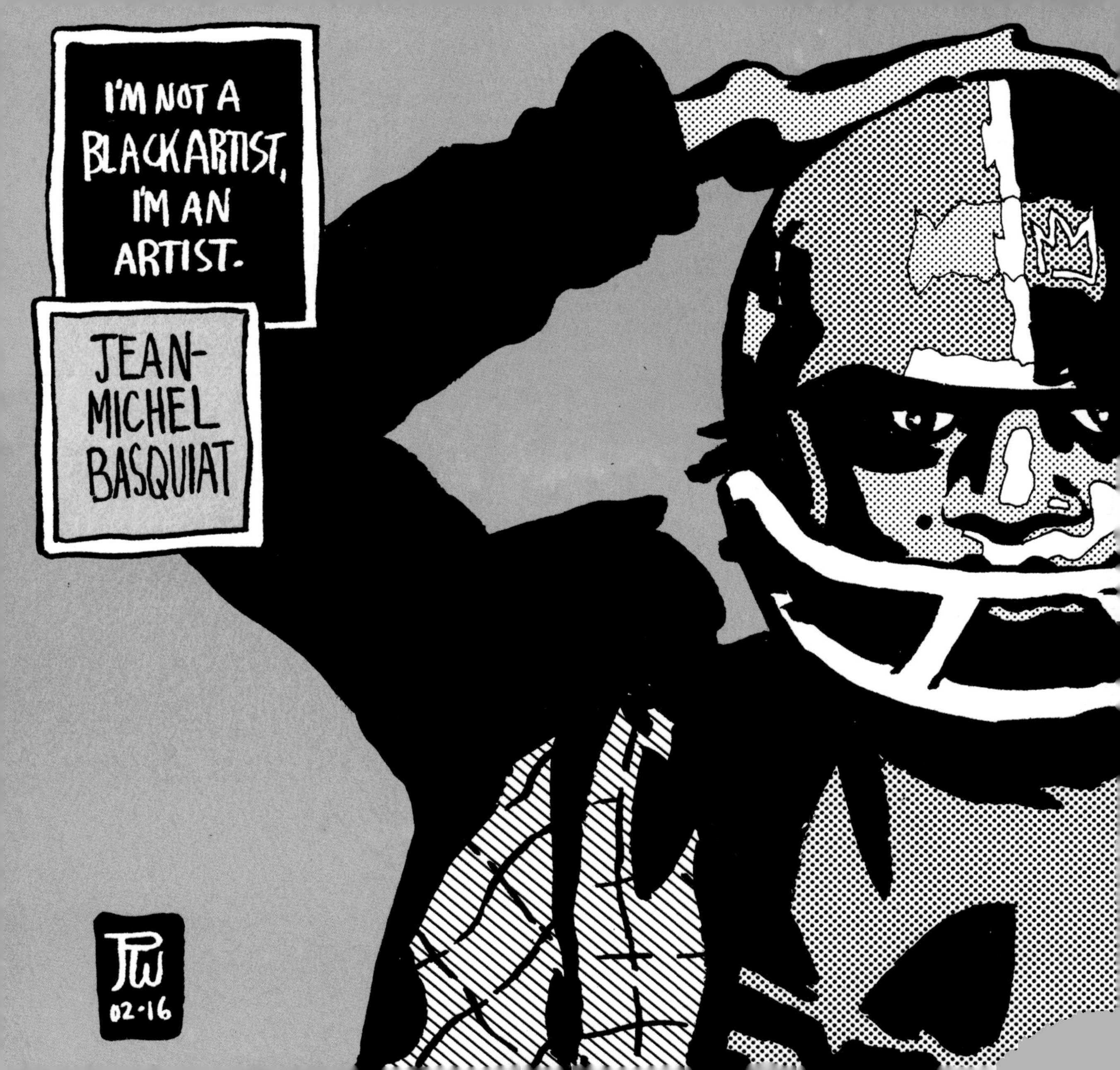
I'M NOT A BLACK ARTIST, I'M AN ARTIST.
JEAN-MICHEL BASQUIAT
PW
02-16

Lee "Scratch" Perry

Audio and style innovator Lee Perry pioneered the dub sound.

Quote taken from a September 2014 interview on *vice.com*.

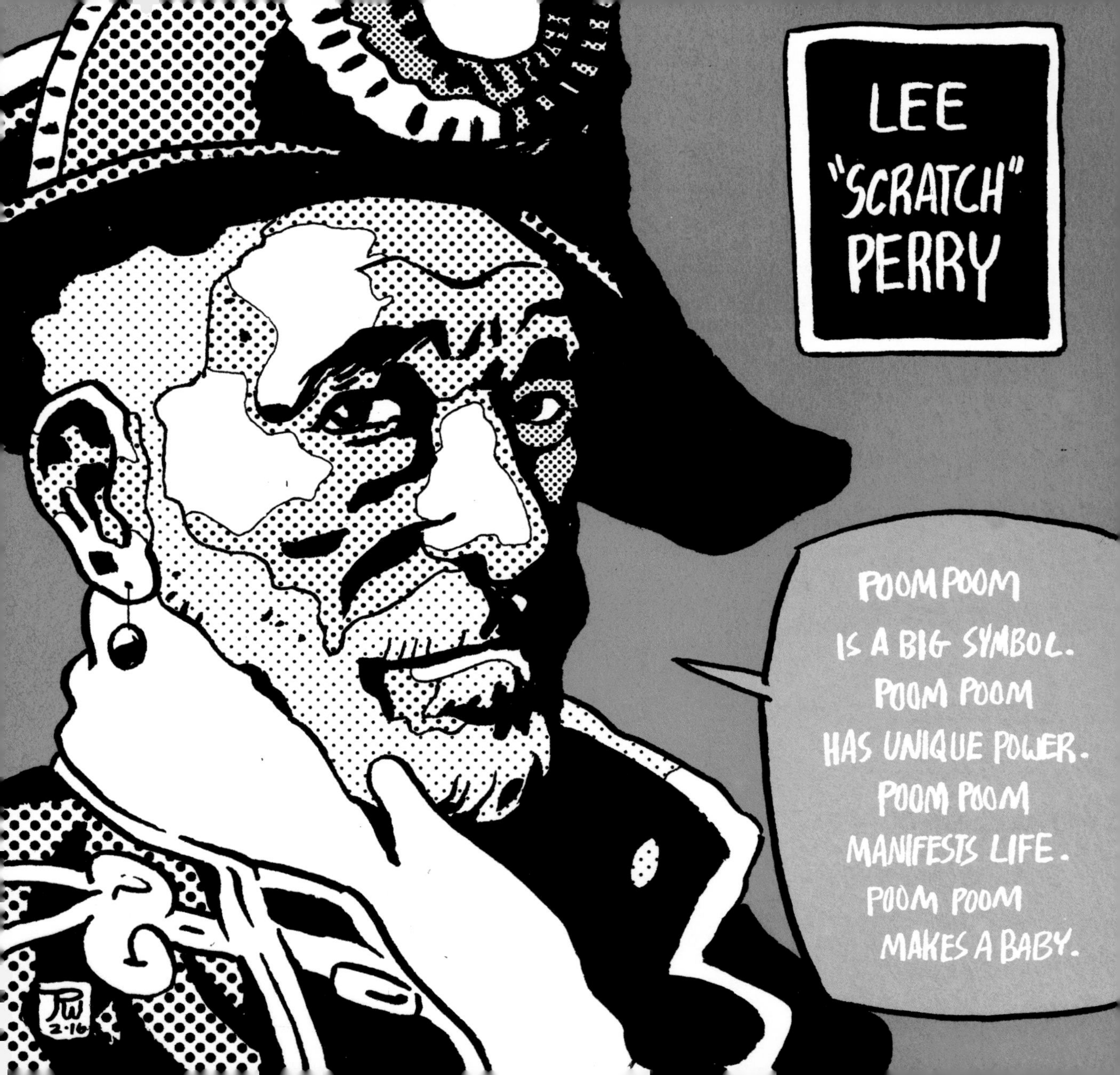
LEE "SCRATCH" PERRY
POOM POOM IS A BIG SYMBOL. POOM POOM HAS UNIQUE POWER. POOM POOM MANIFESTS LIFE. POOM POOM MAKES A BABY.
JW 2·16

Marsha P. Johnson

Sex worker, activist, and cofounder (with Sylvia Rivera) of S.T.A.R. (Street Transgender Action Revolutionaries), Johnson steeled the resistance at Stonewall on June 28 in 1969 when she hurled the "shotglass heard around the world" into a bar mirror, setting off a revolution.

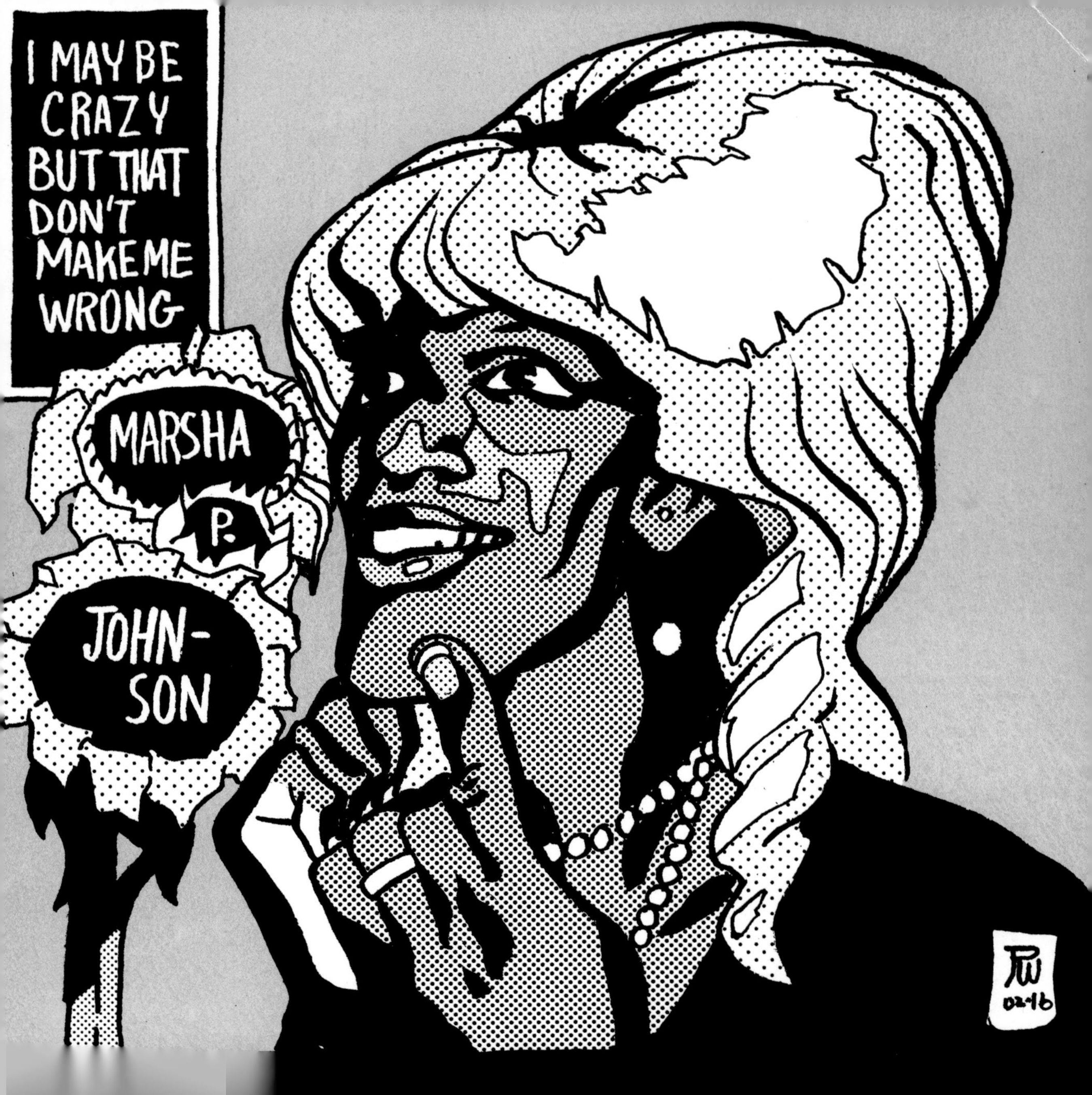
I MAY BE CRAZY BUT THAT DON'T MAKE ME WRONG
MARSHA
P.
JOHN-SON
PW 02-16

2017

Assata Shakur

As a former member of the Black Panther Party and the Black Liberation Army, Assata played a key role in the radical anti-oppression counterculture of the second half of the 20th century. Shakur was the first woman placed on the FBI's Most Wanted list.

Quote taken from *"To My People"* *(July 4, 1973).*

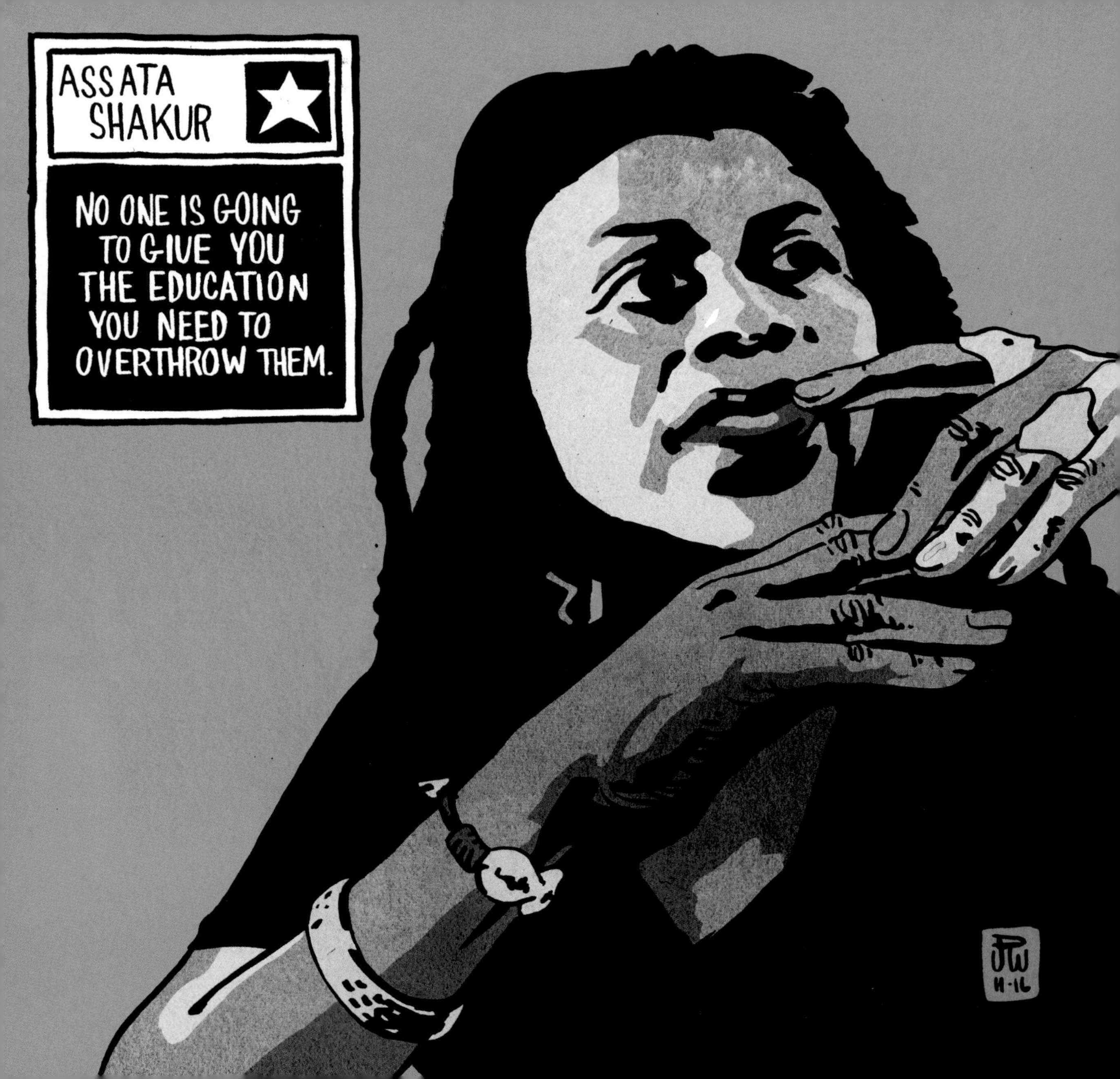
ASSATA SHAKUR
NO ONE IS GOING TO GIVE YOU THE EDUCATION YOU NEED TO OVERTHROW THEM.
JPW 11-16

Prince

Born Prince Rogers Nelson on June 7, 1958, Prince pioneered several sounds in American music, among them New Jack Swing. His work bridged funk, new wave, and psych-rock. His style flew in the face of gender norms and cultural conventions.

Quote taken from an interview in the *New York Times (July 12, 2004)*.

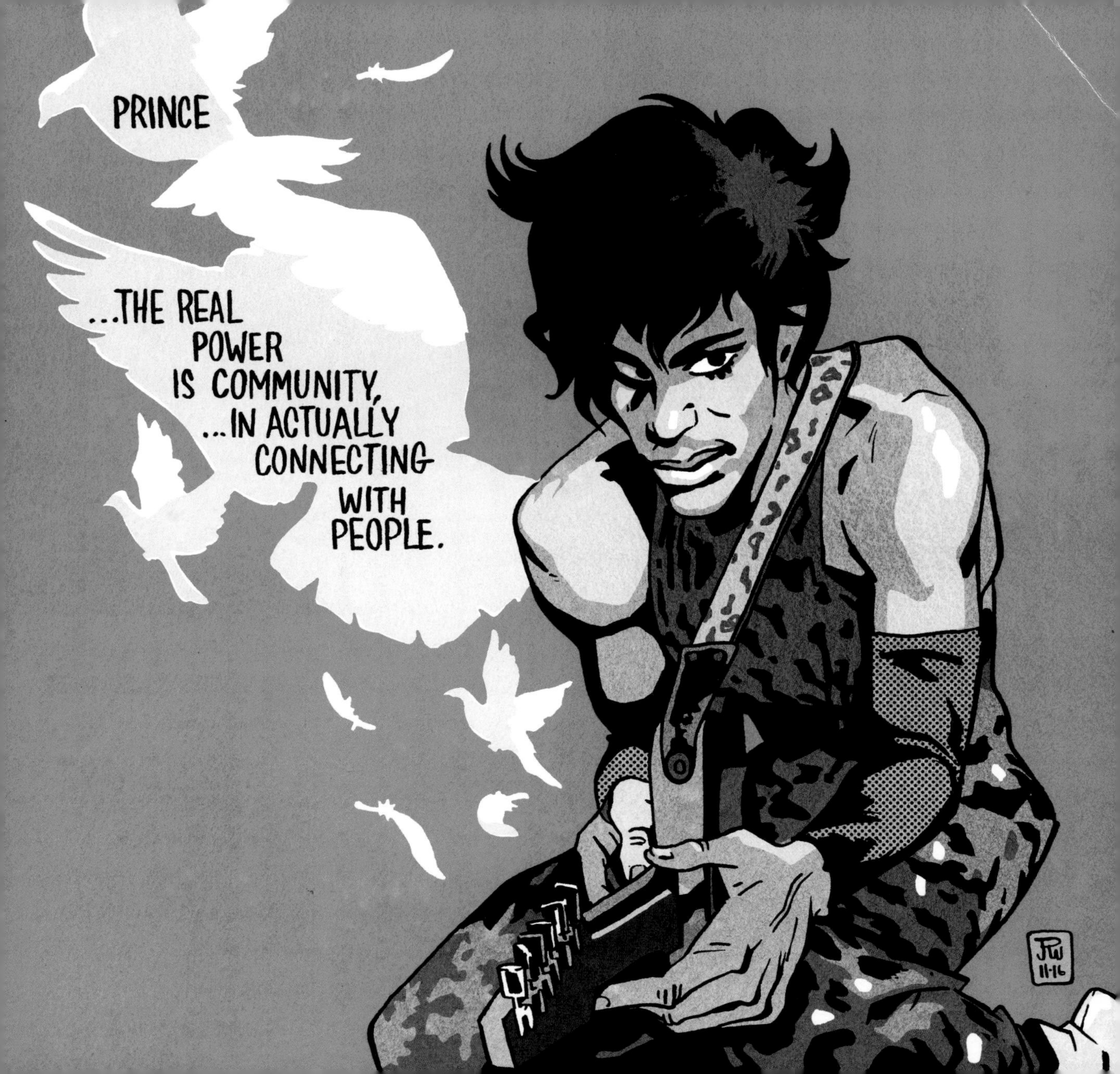
PRINCE
...THE REAL POWER IS COMMUNITY, ...IN ACTUALLY CONNECTING WITH PEOPLE.
JW 11-16

Cathay Williams

When, during the American Civil War, Cathay Williams enlisted in the United States Army as William Cathay, she became the first black woman to serve in the United States armed forces and the only, known on record, to do so as a man.

Quote taken from the *St. Louis Daily Times (January 2, 1876)*.

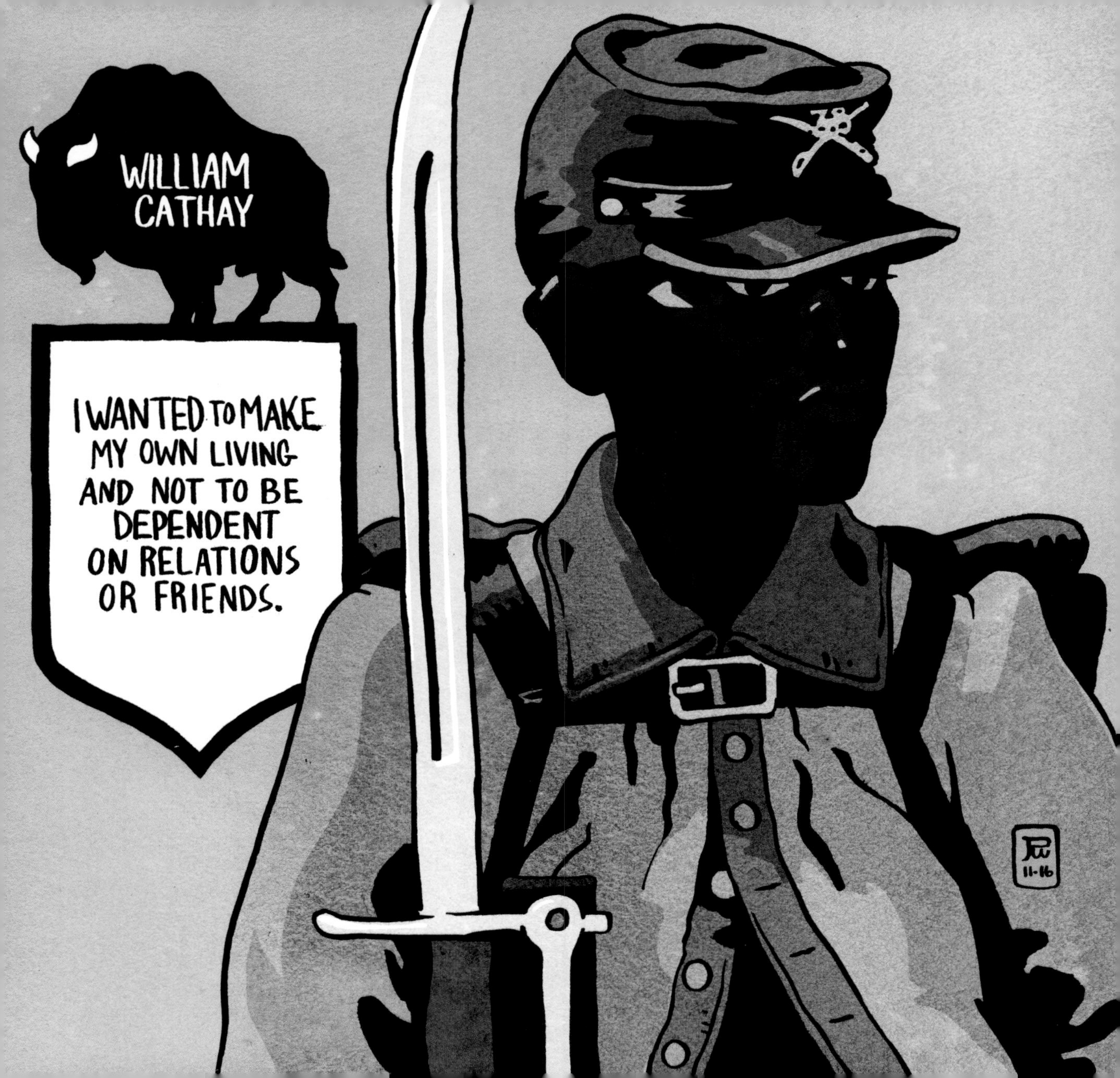
WILLIAM CATHAY
I WANTED TO MAKE MY OWN LIVING AND NOT TO BE DEPENDENT ON RELATIONS OR FRIENDS.
11-16

Nina Simone

Nina Simone was a virtuoso and innovator who addressed structural inequites in her music and in her public life.

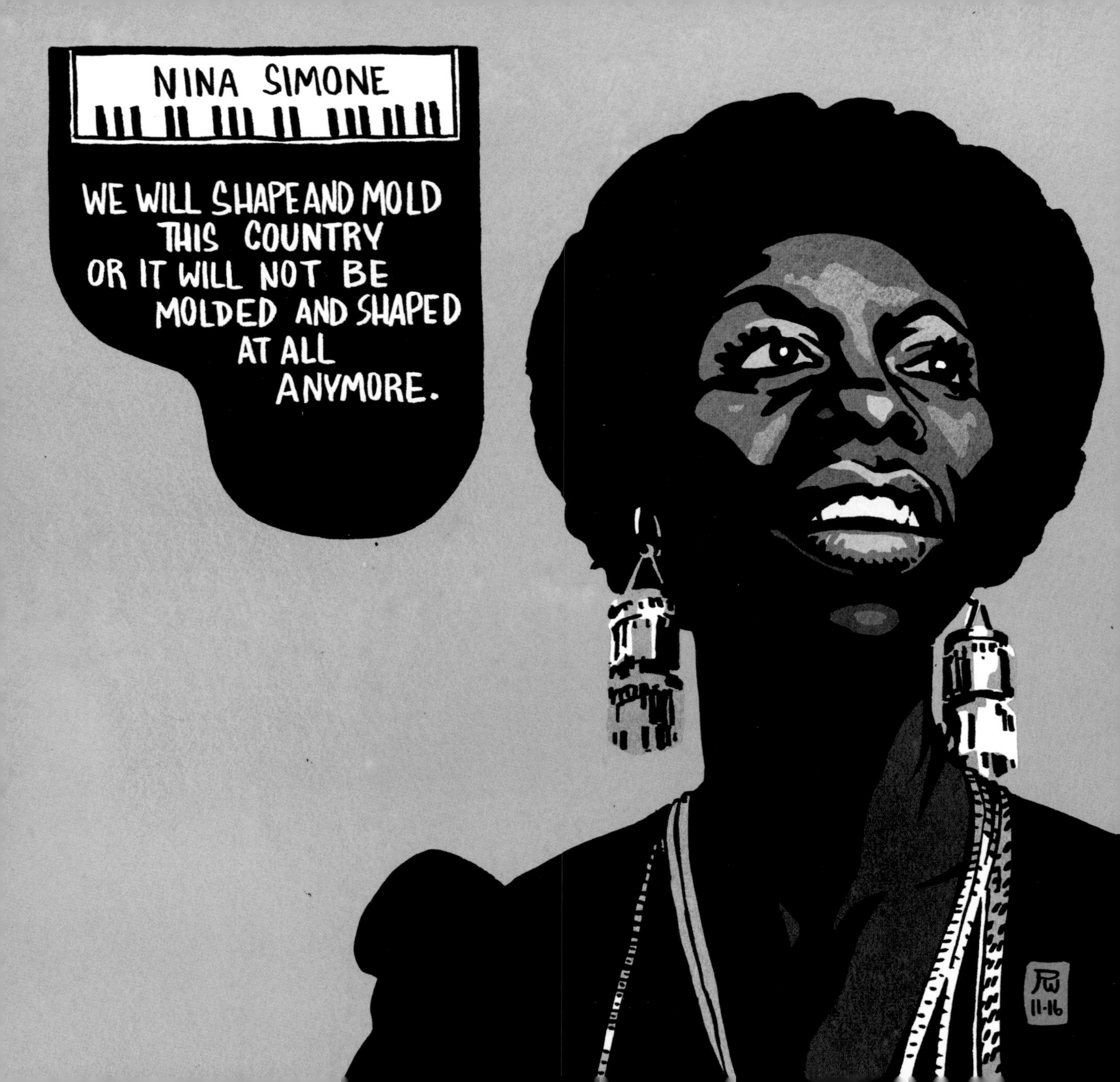
NINA SIMONE
WE WILL SHAPE AND MOLD THIS COUNTRY OR IT WILL NOT BE MOLDED AND SHAPED AT ALL ANYMORE.
RW 11-16

Muhammad Ali

Widely considered "The Greatest", Ali won this title not only because of his exceptional pugilism, but also because of his charisma, eloquence, and civil rights activism.

Quote taken from *Time Magazine (February 27, 1978).*

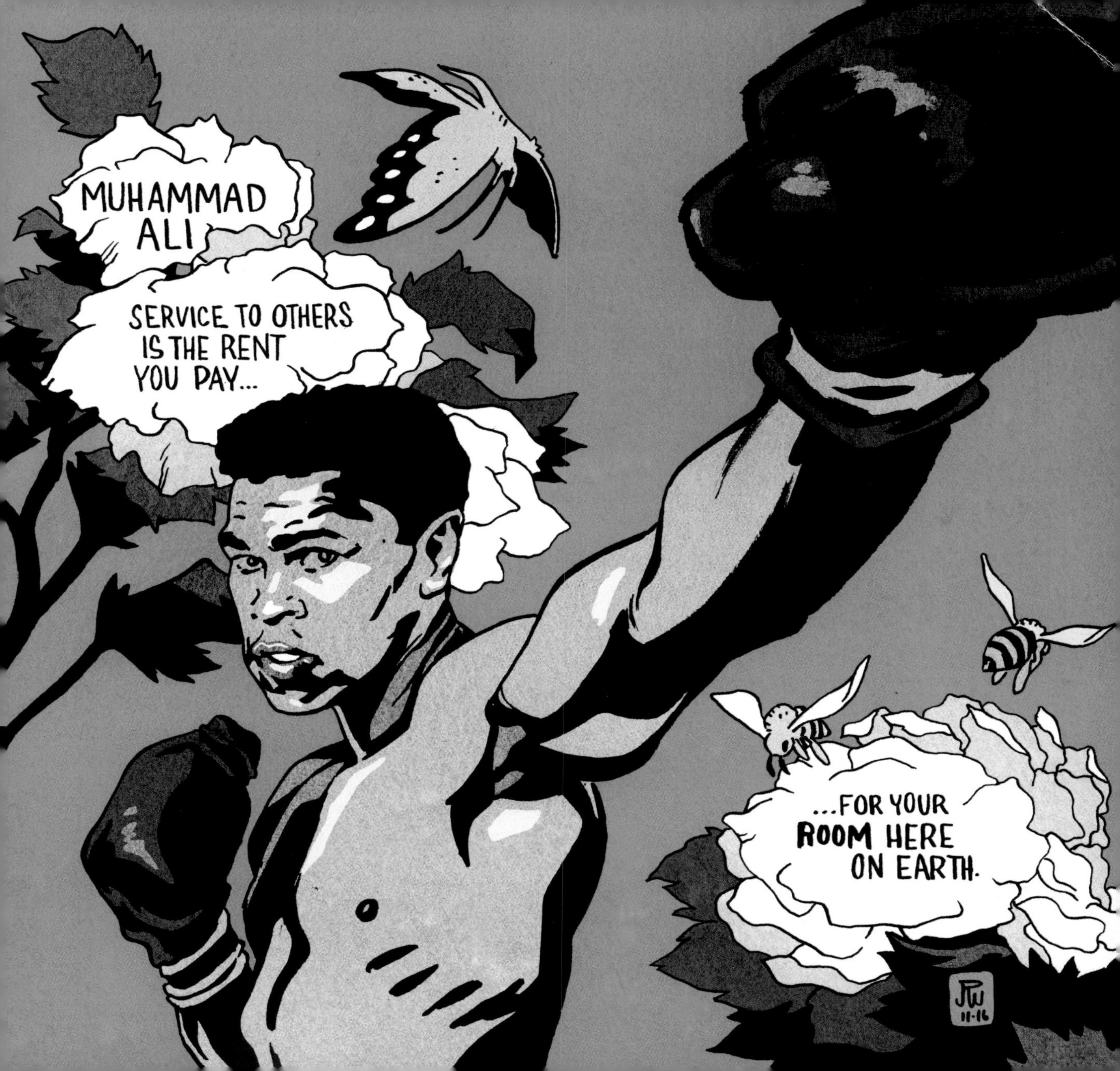
MUHAMMAD ALI
SERVICE TO OTHERS IS THE RENT YOU PAY...
...FOR YOUR ROOM HERE ON EARTH.
JPW 11-16

Young M.A.

Young M.A.'s adroit use of language pushes the boundaries of New York Rap's hedonistic and nihilistic lyricist tradition while upholding black street culture's progressive standard regarding identity and sexuality.

Quote taken from her 2016 single, "OOOUUU."

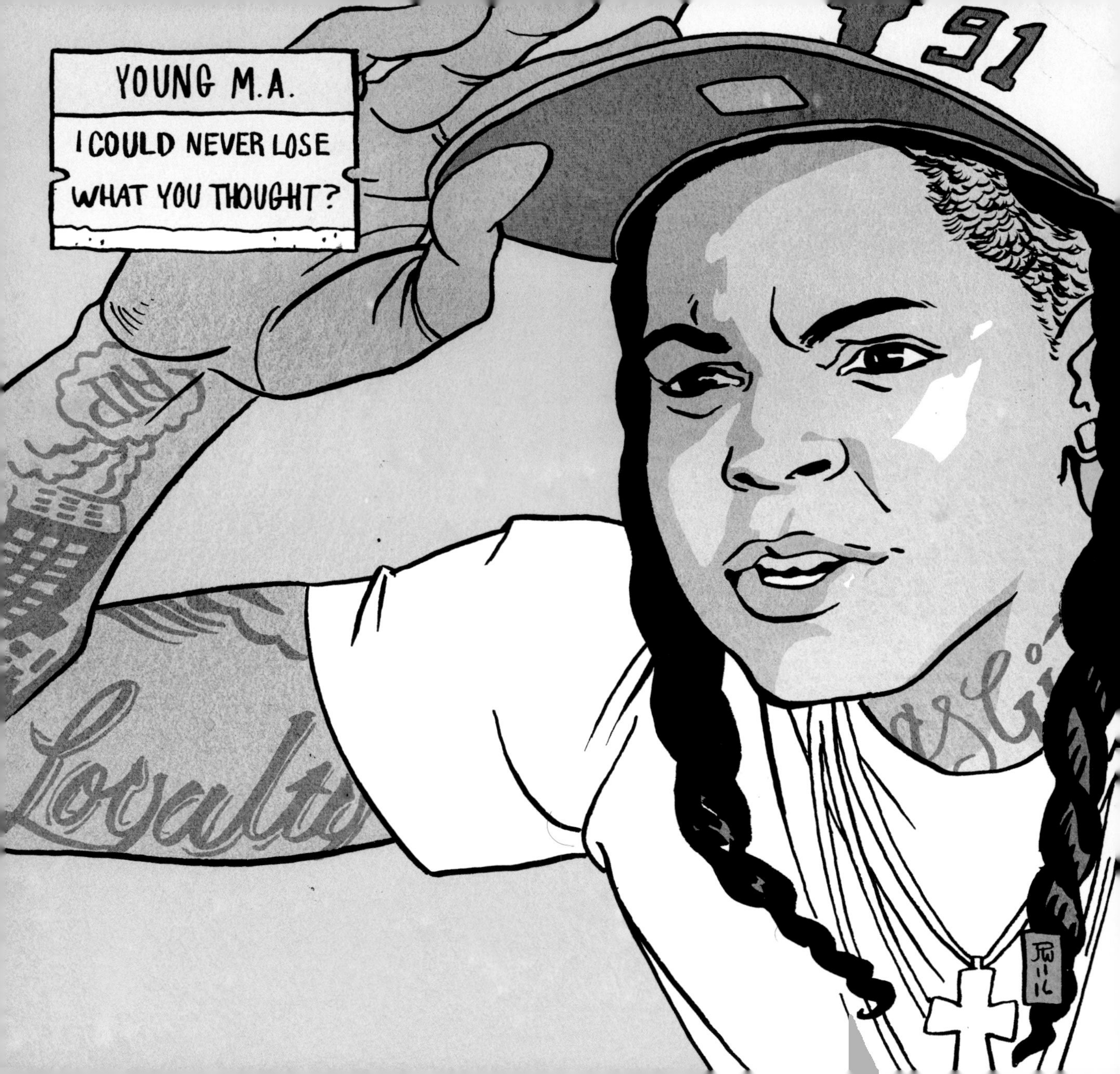
YOUNG M.A.
I COULD NEVER LOSE
WHAT YOU THOUGHT?
91
Loyalty

Sojourner Truth

After liberating herself and her infant daughter from slavery in 1826, Sojourner Truth fought and won the freedom of her son, from a white man, becoming the first slave in American history to do so.

She continued to fight slavery and sexism, and was one of the first to address this intersection of oppression.

Quote taken from *Narrative of Sojourner Truth: A Northern Slave... (1850)*.

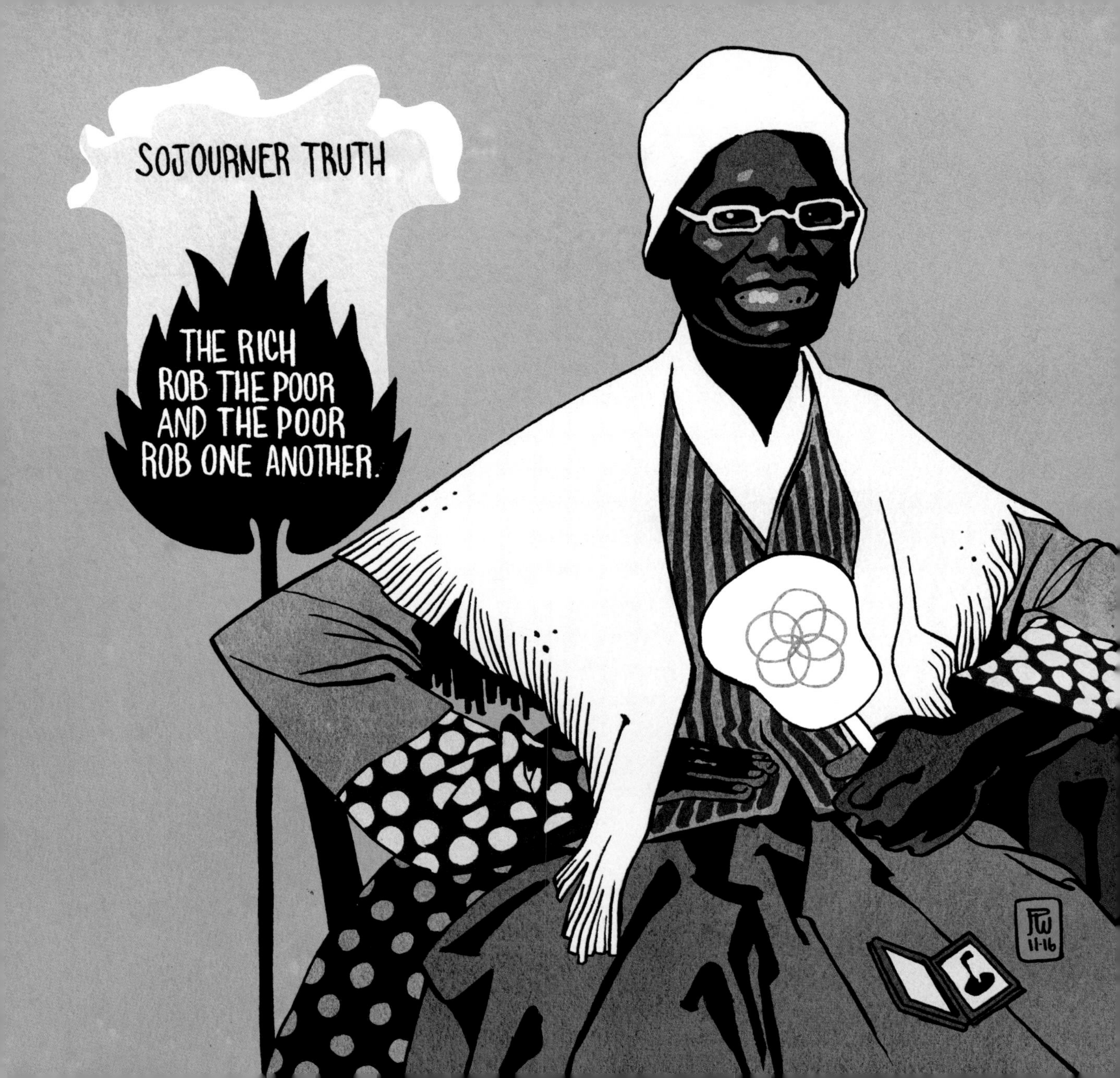
SOJOURNER TRUTH
THE RICH
ROB THE POOR
AND THE POOR
ROB ONE ANOTHER.
PW
11-16

Cheryl Dunye

Filmmaker Cheryl Dunye captured intersectional theory in celluloid. Her humanizing lens broke new ground in cinema.

Quote taken from the 1996 film *Watermelon Woman.*

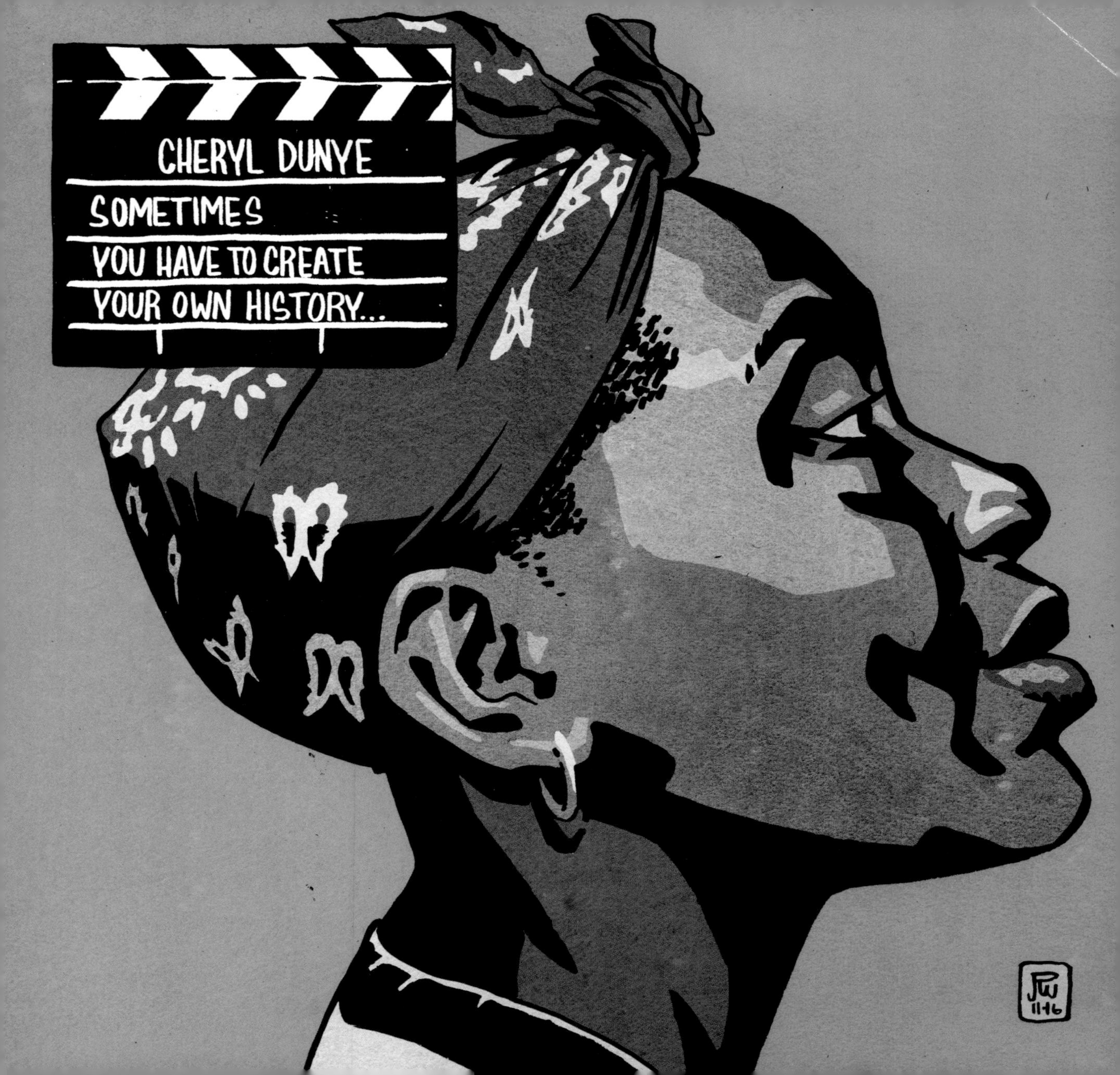
CHERYL DUNYE
SOMETIMES
YOU HAVE TO CREATE
YOUR OWN HISTORY...
JW
11-16

Emory Douglas

Minister of Culture for the Black Panther Party for Self Defense, Emory Douglas developed an aesthetic for the revoltion. He continues to actively pursue justice and human rights internationally.

Quote taken from an April 2015 interview in *Print Magazine.*

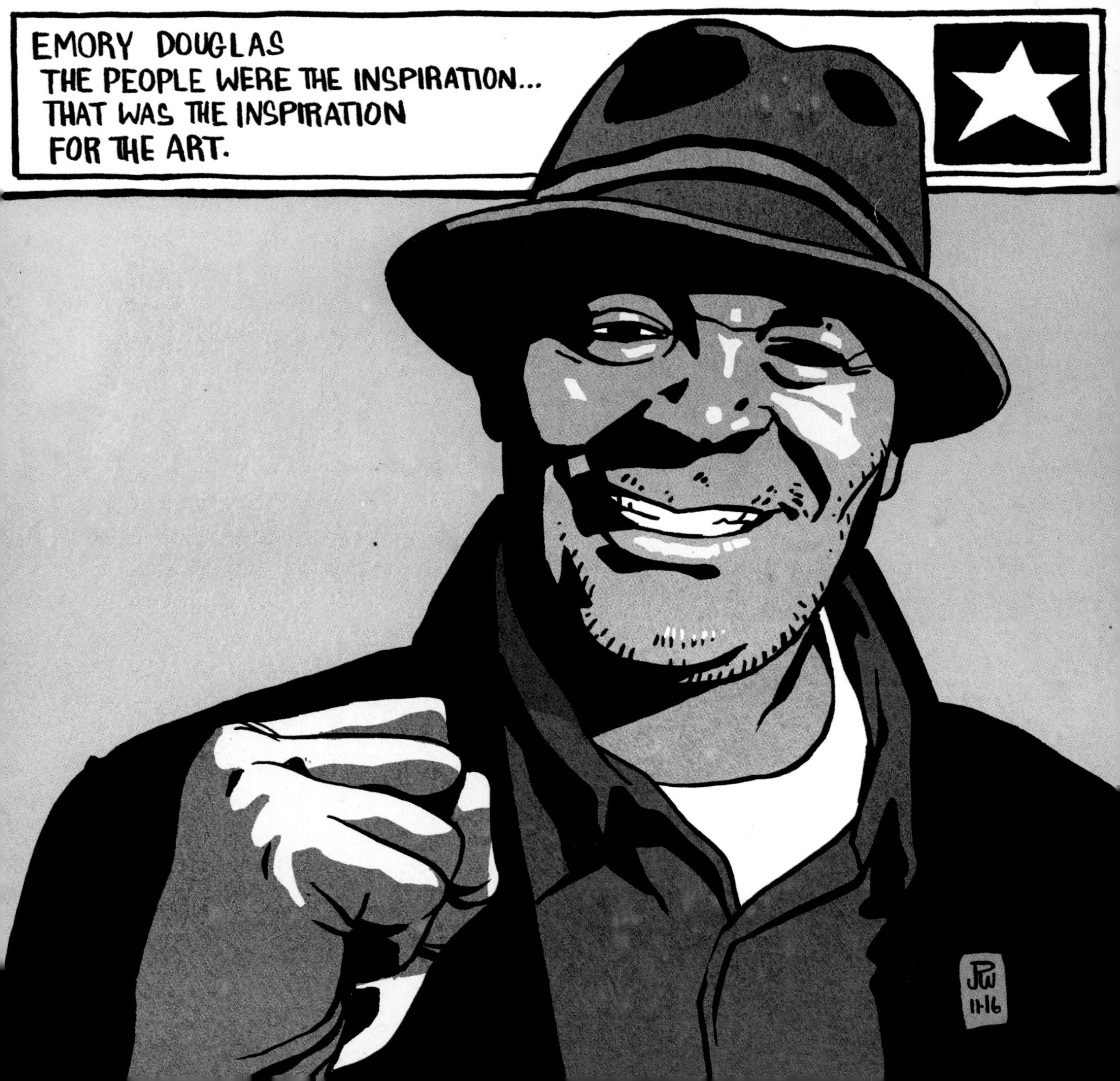
EMORY DOUGLAS
THE PEOPLE WERE THE INSPIRATION... THAT WAS THE INSPIRATION FOR THE ART.
JPW 11-16

RAMM:ΣLL:ZΣΣ

Rammellzee's work in music, graffiti, and conceptual art embodied what has become afro-futurism and was an essential part of the downtown New York scene of the late '70s-'80s. Rammellzee developed Gothic Futurist theory, a deconstruction of language.

Quote taken from *ICONIC TREATISE GOTHIC FUTURISM (1979)*.

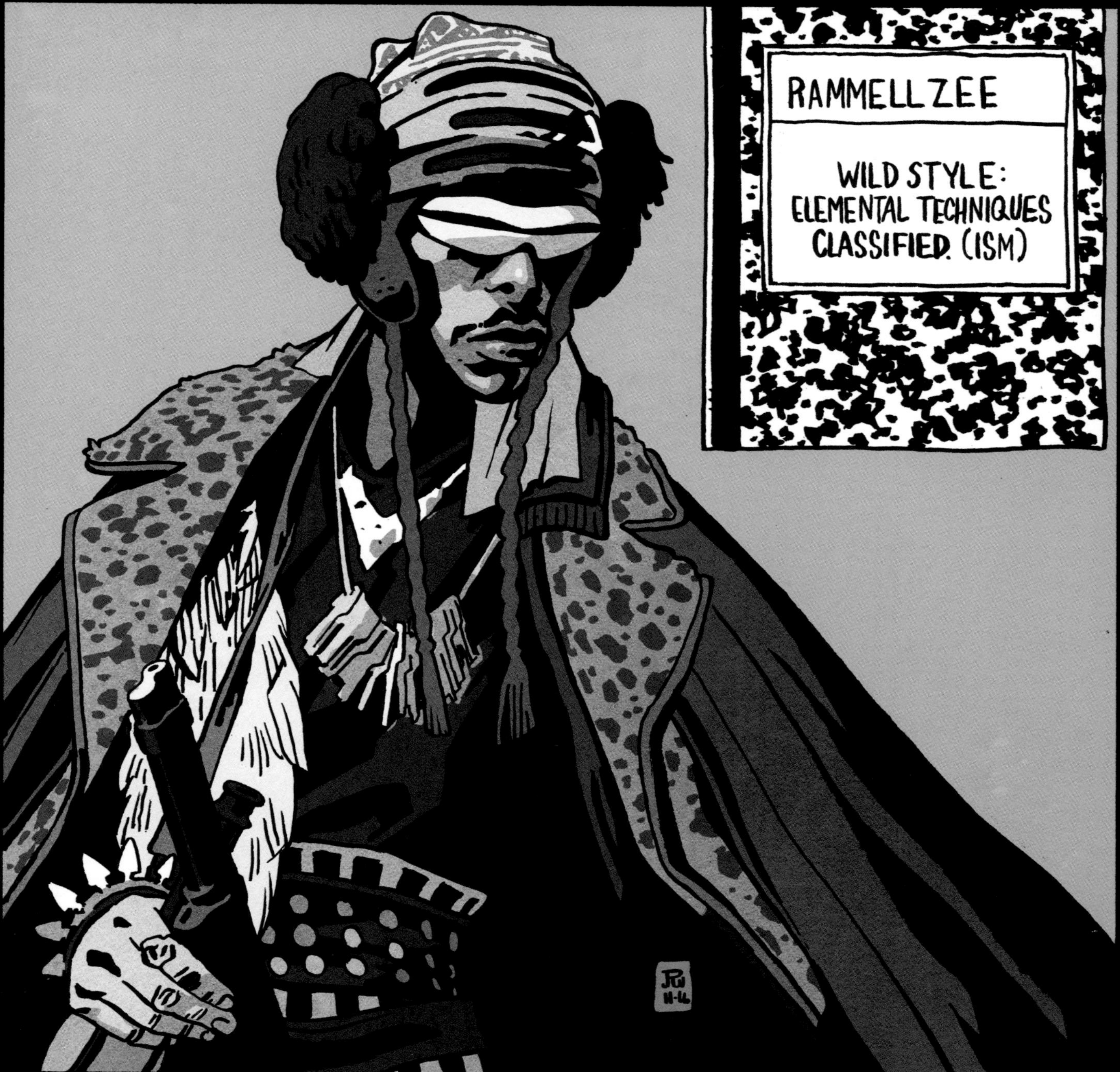
RAMMELLZEE
WILD STYLE:
ELEMENTAL TECHNIQUES
CLASSIFIED. (ISM)

Jimi Hendrix

Widely considered the god of electric guitar, Jimi Hendrix's innovative use of the instrument pushed the boundaries of not just the instrument but the nature of the application of sound and feedback in music. His sound is the missing link between psych-rock, heavy metal, funk, and neo-soul.

Quote taken from *Associated Press Archives: 1970 Interview NY City.*

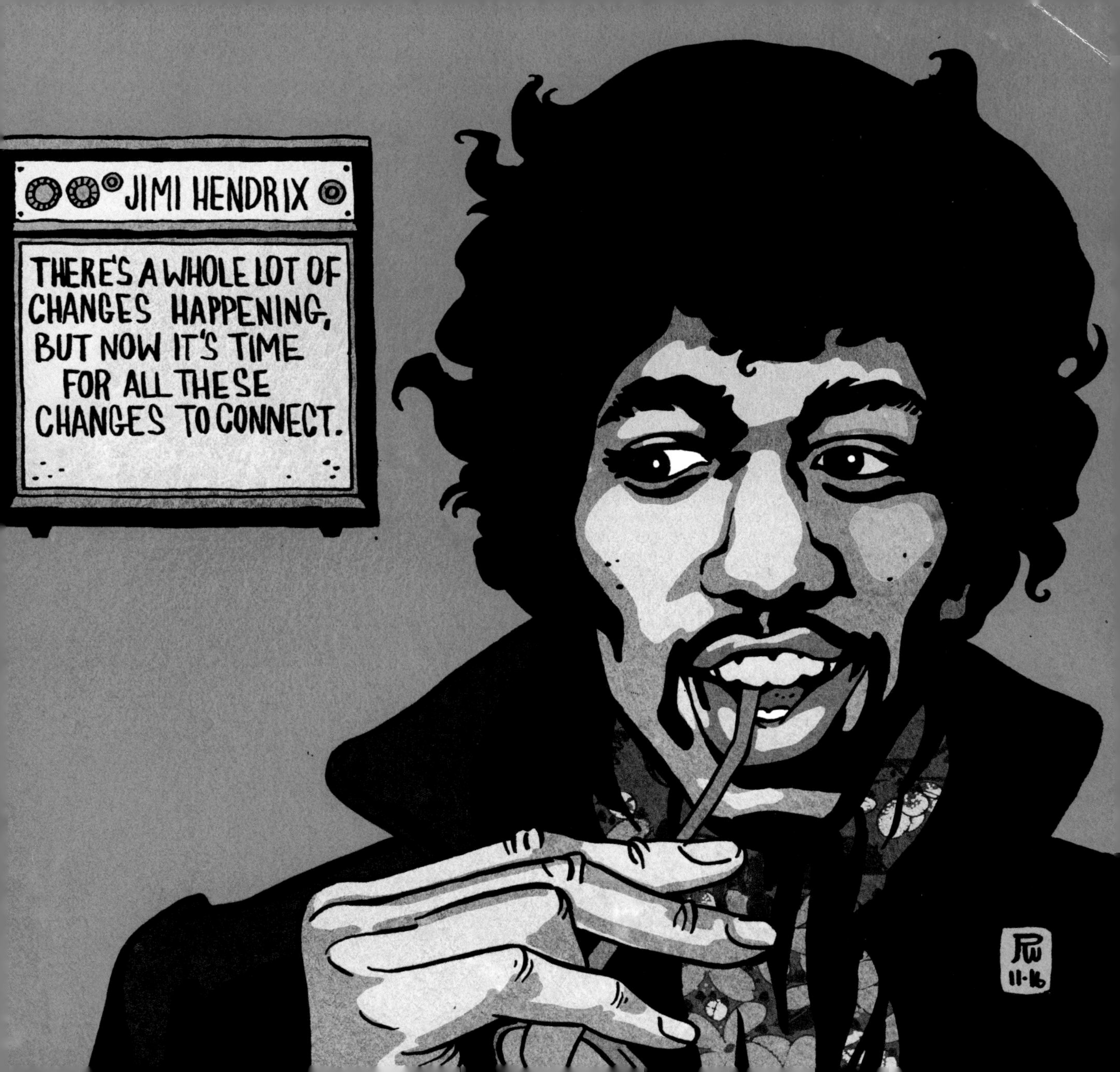
JIMI HENDRIX
THERE'S A WHOLE LOT OF CHANGES HAPPENING, BUT NOW IT'S TIME FOR ALL THESE CHANGES TO CONNECT.
PW 11-16

Katherine Johnson

Physicist and mathematician, Katherine Johnson's math put a man on the moon. Her computations lent credibility to the application of early computers in the American space program.

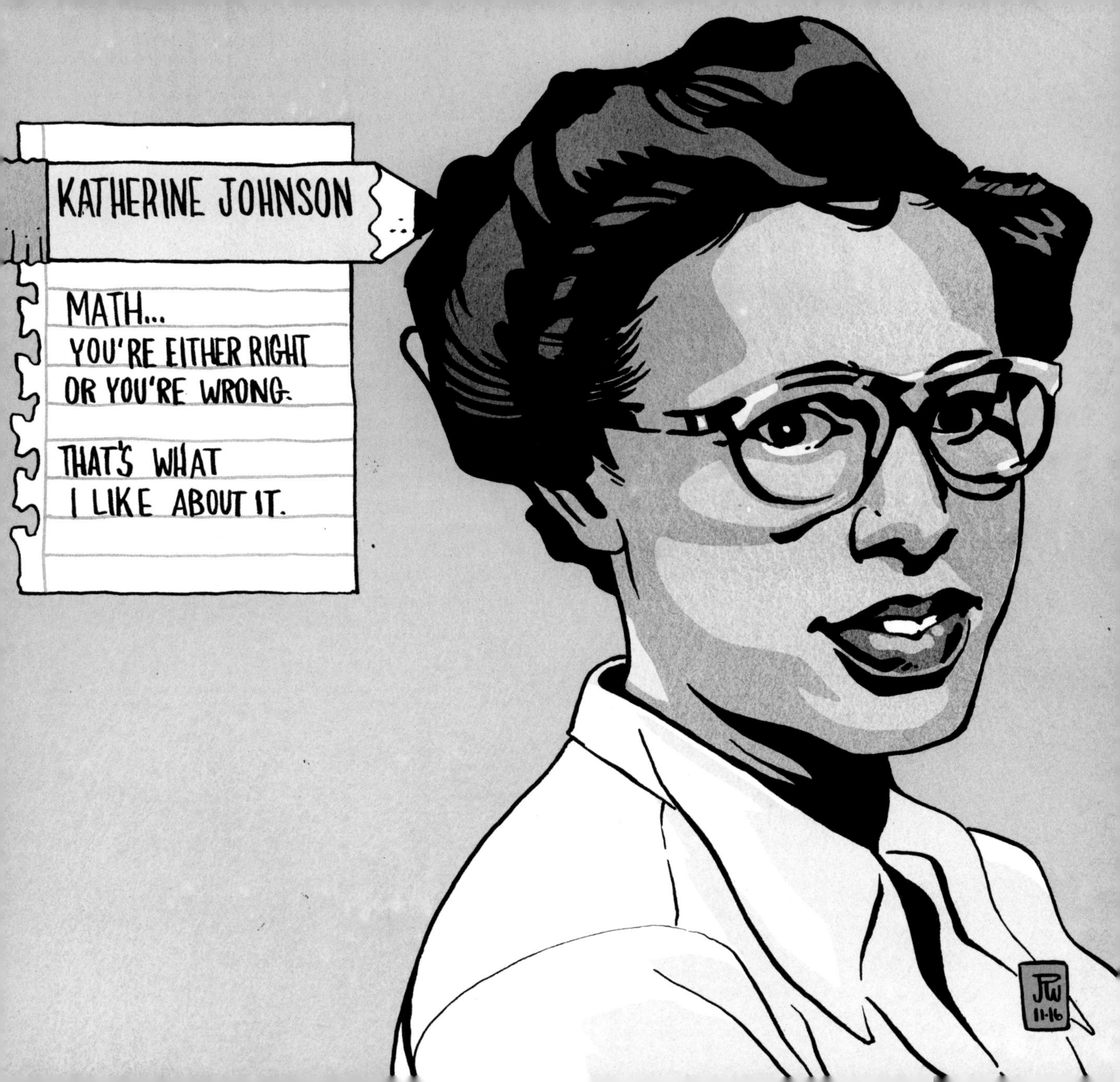
KATHERINE JOHNSON
MATH...
YOU'RE EITHER RIGHT
OR YOU'RE WRONG.
THAT'S WHAT
I LIKE ABOUT IT.
JPW
11-16

Mary Ellen Pleasant

Pioneering entrepreneur, Mary Ellen Pleasant, collaborated on the Underground Railroad. She used her economic success to fund the abolition movement, including the activism of John Brown.

Quote taken from *Ebony Magazine, April 1979, "The Mystery of Mary Ellen Pleasant."*

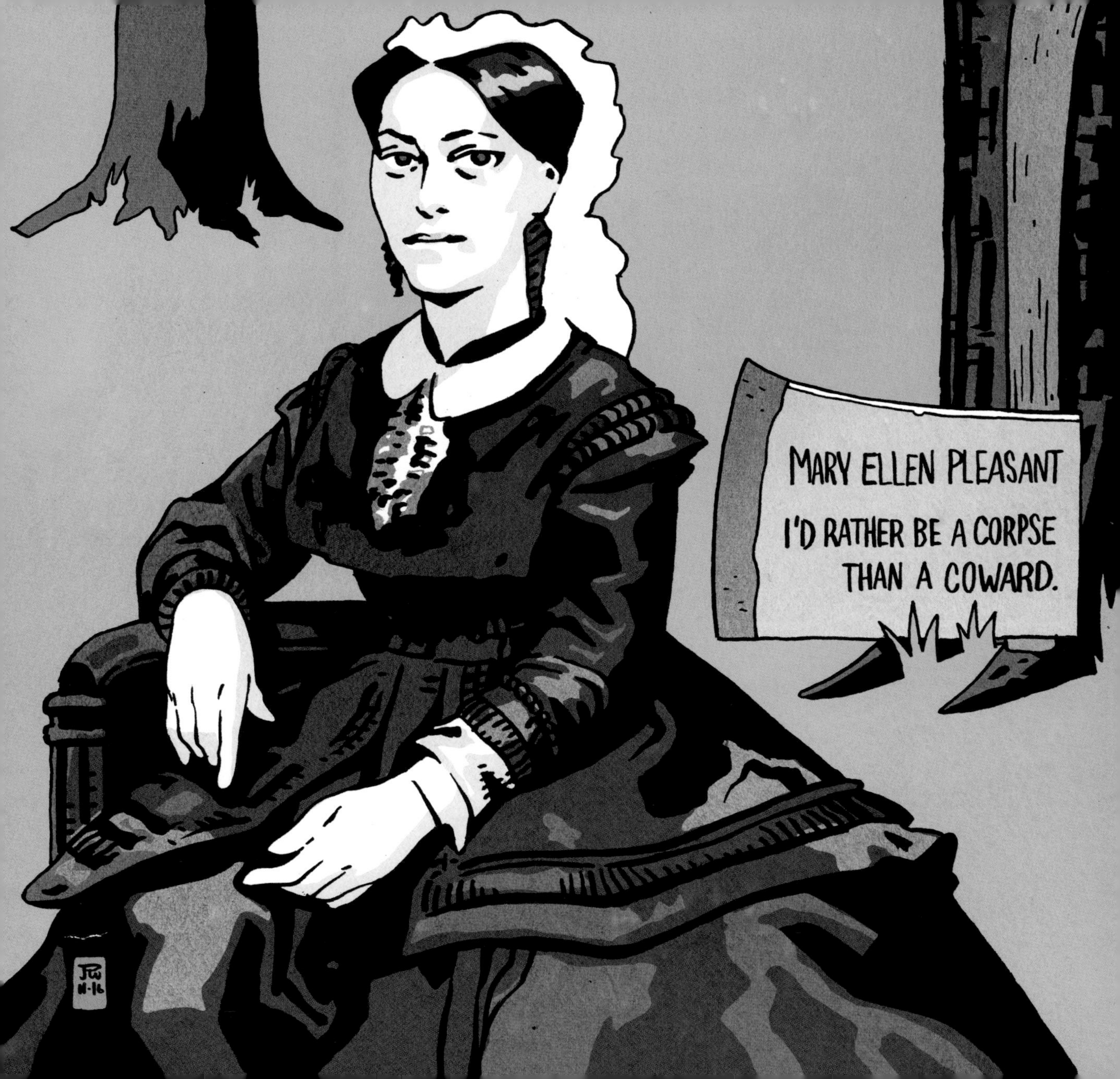
MARY ELLEN PLEASANT
I'D RATHER BE A CORPSE THAN A COWARD.

Eugene Bullard

A refugee of American Jim Crow terrorism, Eugene Bullard fled to Europe where he became the hero Europe never asked for and that America didn't deserve. Bullard earned a Croix de Guerre flying for the French in WWI and served as a spy for the French Resistance in WWII.

Quote taken from the side of his aircraft.

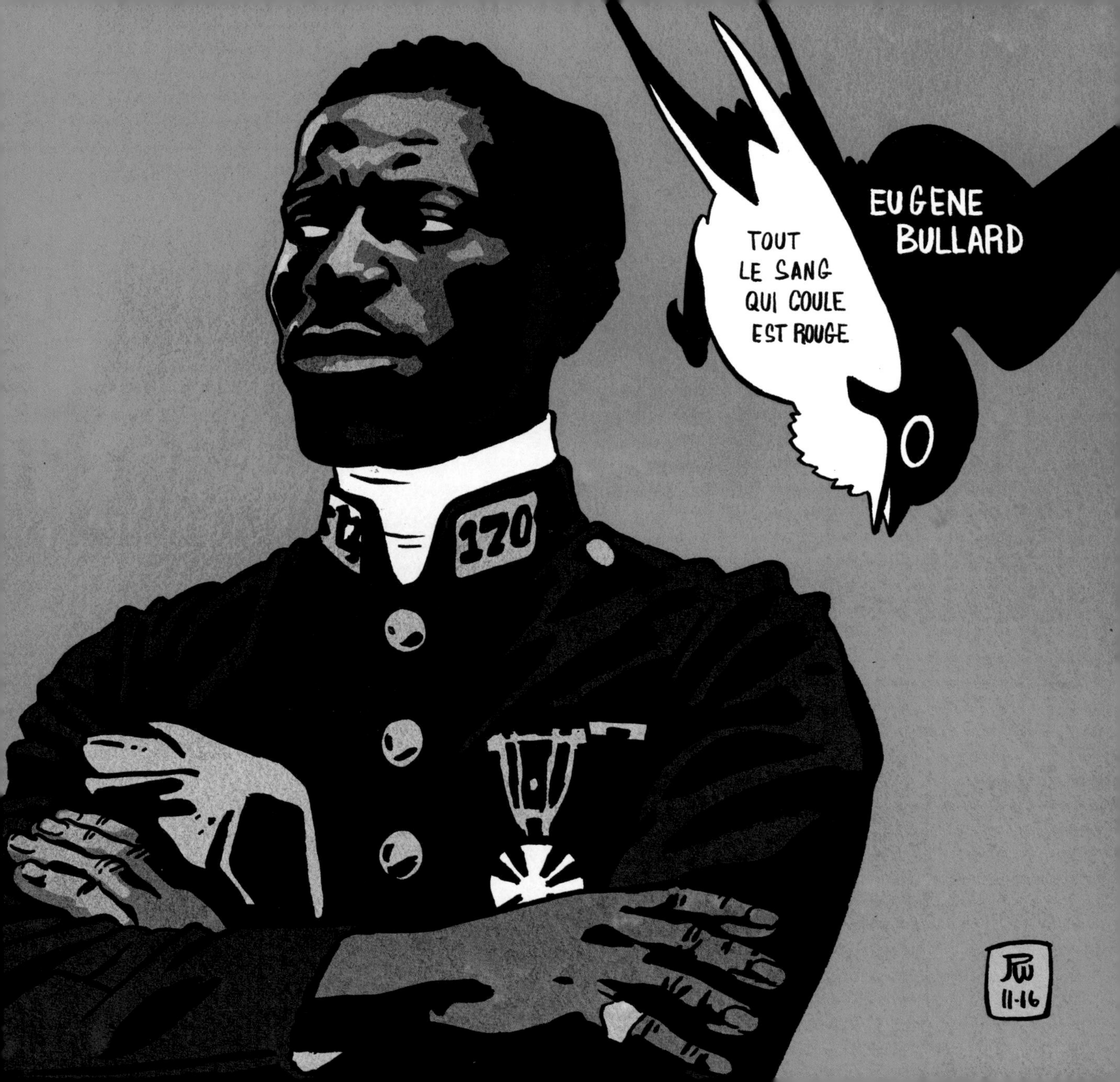
EUGENE BULLARD
TOUT LE SANG QUI COULE EST ROUGE
170
JW 11-16

bell hooks

Author, activist, and intellectual, bell hooks' work explores how structural racism, gender inequality, sexism, and economic inequity intersect to form an oppressive matrix.

Quote taken from *CNN Books, "bell hooks: A chat with the Author of 'All About Love: New Visions'"* (February 17, 2000).

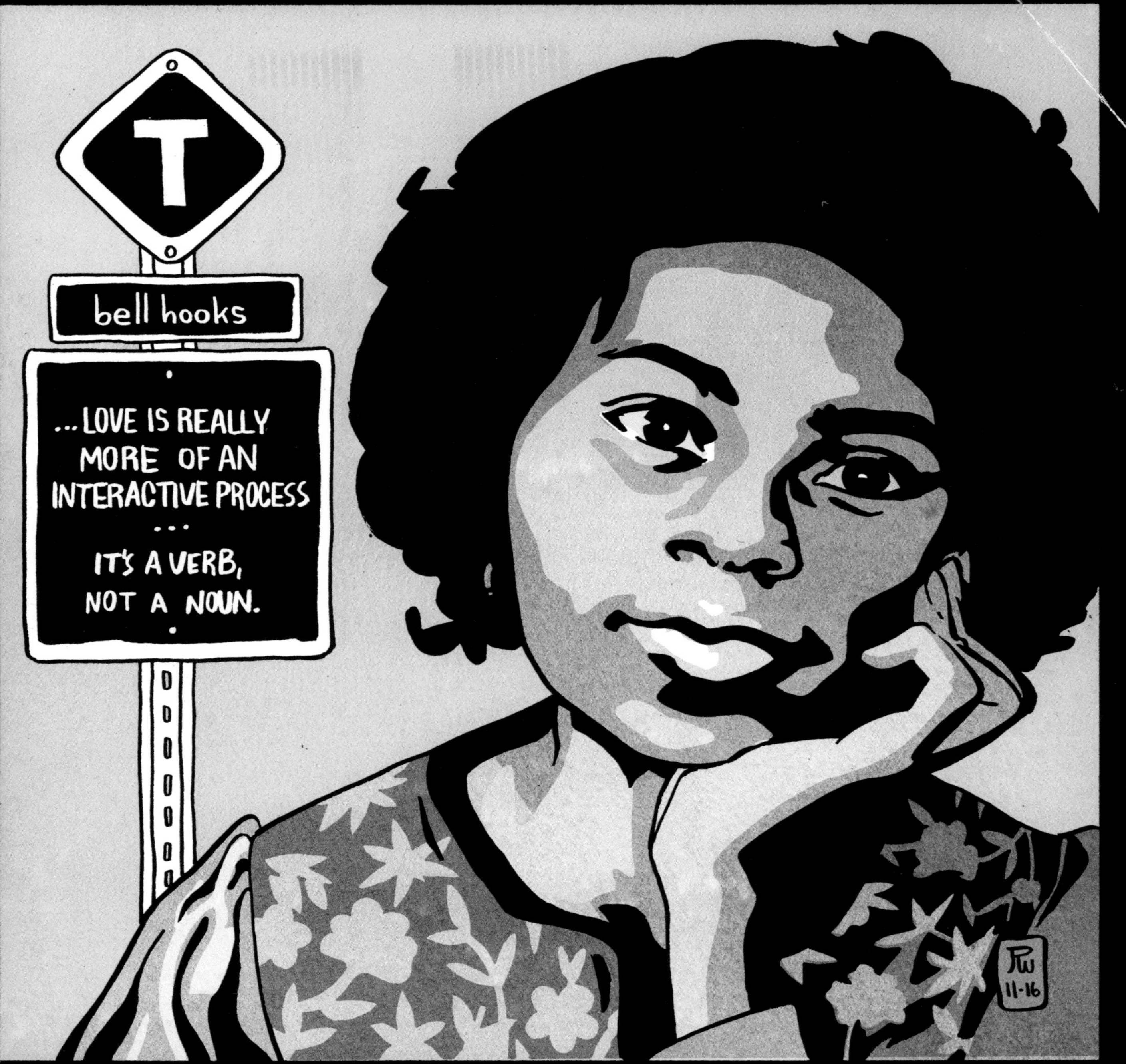
T
bell hooks
...LOVE IS REALLY MORE OF AN INTERACTIVE PROCESS
...
IT'S A VERB, NOT A NOUN.
PW 11-16

WORKS CITED

ANGELA DAVIS
Davis, Angela. Women, Culture and Politics. New York: Vintage, 1989.

MC RIDE
Death Grips. "Beware." Exmilitary. 2011.

GEORGE JOSEPH HERRIMAN
"George Herriman." Los Angeles Review of Books. Los Angeles: LARB, 2016. Web. December 5, 2016. <https://lareviewofbooks.org/author-page/george-herriman/#!>.

ICE CUBE
Luscombe, Belinda. "10 Questions with Ice Cube." Time Magazine, June 12, 2014. Web. December 5, 2016. <http://time.com/2863202/10-questions-with-ice-cube/>.

SAUL WILLIAMS
Williams, Saul. "All Coltrane Solos At Once" feat. Haleek Maul. MartyrLoserKing. Fader Label, 2016.

DAVE CHAPPELLE
Inside the Actors Studio. "Dave Chappelle." Season 12, Episode 7. Hosted by James Lipton. Bravo Cable, February 12, 2006.

SPIKE LEE
Lee, Spike. Lecture at Pratt Institute. New York: February 25, 2014.

ARTURO ALFONSO SCHOMBURG
Schomburg, Arturo. "The Negro Digs Up His Past." Survey Graphic, Vol. VI, No. 6, March 1925, edited by Alain Locke. Black Classic Press, 1925.

LAVERNE COX
Kevin Fallon. "Laverne Cox Talks Love, Healing, and Pride." The Daily Beast, June 14, 2016. The Daily Beast Company, 2016. Web. December 5, 2016. <http://www.thedailybeast.com/articles/2016/06/15/laverne-cox-talks-love-healing-and-pride.html>.

JAMES BALDWIN
Baldwin, James. "The Negro's Role in American Culture." Negro Digest, March 1962. Johnson Publishing Company.

AUDRE LORDE
Lorde, Audre. "The Master's Tools Will Never Dismantle the Master's House." Sister Outsider: Essays and Speeches. Crossing Press, 1984.

LENA HORNE
Young, Courtney. "Farewell to Ms. Lena." Ms.Magazine.com. May 11, 2010. 2016. Web. December 5, 2016. <http://msmagazine.com/blog/2010/05/11/farewell-to-ms-lena/>.

KIMBERLY BRYANT
Forde, Brian. "Connecting Kids from Diverse Backgrounds to Tech Skills." The White house. The United States Government, February 28, 2014. Web. December 5, 2016. <https://www.whitehouse.gov/blog/2014/02/28/connecting-kids-diverse-backgrounds-tech-skills>.

FRED HAMPTON
The Murder of Fred Hampton. Directed by Howard Alk. Film. Chicago: The Chicago Film Group, 1971.

SERENA WILLIAMS
"18 inspiring quotes from badass female Olympians." Marie Claire, August 11, 2016. Time Inc, 2016. Web. December 5, 2016. <http://www.marieclaire.co.uk/entertainment/people/olympic-quotes-254439/>.

POLY STYRENE
X-Ray Spex. "Oh Bondage Up Yours!" Virgin, September 1977.

Uncut Magazine, Issue 164, January 2011.

MYKKI BLANCO
Battan, Carrie. "We Invented Swag: NYC's Queer Rap." Pitchfork, March 21, 2012. Condé Nast, 2016. Web. December 5, 2016. <http://pitchfork.com/features/article/8793-we-invented-swag/>.

OCTAVIA BUTLER
"Octavia Butler, Science Fiction Writer." African American Registry. African American Registry, 2013. Web. December 5, 2016. <http://www.aaregistry.org/historic_events/view/octavia-butler-science-fiction-writer/>.

ZADIE SMITH
Smith, Zadie. White Teeth. New York: Vintage, 2001.

KANYE WEST
ASAP Rocky. "Jukebox Joints" feat. Joe Fox and Kanye West. At. Long. Last. ASAP. A$AP Worldwide, Polo Grounds Music, RCA Records, 2015.

SHIRLEY CHISHOLM
Chisholm, Shirley. Unbought and Unbossed. Boston, Massachusetts: Take Root Media, 2010.

JEAN-MICHEL BASQUIAT
"Jean-Michel Basquiat Biography." The Biography.com, July 25, 2014. A&E Television Networks, 2016. Web. December 5, 2016. <http://www.biography.com/people/jean-michel-basquiat-185851>.

LEE "SCRATCH" PERRY
Lhooq, Michelle. "Lee 'Scratch' Perry is the World's Most Badass 78-Year-Old." Thump.vice.com, September 24, 2014. Vice Media, 2016. Web. December 5, 2016. <https://thump.vice.com/en_au/article/lee-scratch-perry-is-the-worlds-most-badass-78-year-old>.

ASSATA SHAKUR
Shakur, Assata. "To My People." Radio address, July 4, 1973. From Assata: An Autobiography. Chicago, Illinois: Lawrence Hill Books, 2001.

PRINCE
Pareles, Jon. "For Prince, A Resurgence Accompanied By Spirituality." The New York Times. July 12, 2004. Web. December 5, 2016. <http://www.nytimes.com/2004/07/12/arts/for-prince-a-resurgence-accompanied-by-spirituality.html?_r=0>.

CATHAY WILLIAMS
Engel, Kerilynn. "Cathay Williams, AKA William Cathay, American Civil War soldier." Amazingwomeninhistory.com, June 9, 2013. Amazing Women in History. Web. December 5, 2016. <http://www.amazingwomeninhistory.com/cathay-williams/>.

NINA SIMONE
Light, Alan. What Happened, Miss Simone? RadicalMedia, 2016. New York: Crown Archetype, 2016.

MUHAMMAD ALI
"The Greatest is Gone." Time Magazine, February 27, 1978. Time Inc, 2016. Web. December 5, 2016. <http://content.time.com/time/magazine/article/0,9171,919377,00.html>.

YOUNG M.A.
Young M.A. "OOOUUU." U-Dub, 2016.

SOJOURNER TRUTH
Truth, Sojourner. Narrative of Sojourner Truth. Edited by Olive Gilbert. Boston: 1850.

CHERYL DUNYE
Dunye, Cheryl. Watermelon Woman. Film. New York: First Run Features, 1966.

EMORY DOUGLAS
Boyd, Natalie. "2015 AIGA Medalist Emory Douglas." Print Magazine, April 20, 2015. F+W, 2016. Web. December 5, 2016. <http://www.printmag.com/article/2015-aiga-winner-emory-douglas/>.

RAMMELLZEE
Rammellzee. "Iconic Treatise Gothic Futurism." 1979. Accessed from post.thing.net. The Thing, Inc. Web. December 5, 2016. <http://post.thing.net/node/3086>.

JIMI HENDRIX
Jimi Hendrix Electric Church. Directed by John McDermott. New York: Showtime, 2015.

KATHERINE JOHNSON
"Women in STEMP: How Katherine Johnson Took Her Skills to the Moon." Base 11, February 26, 2016. Base 11, 2016. Web. December 5, 2016. <http://www.base11.com/women-in-stem-how-katherine-johnson-took-her-skills-to-the-moon/>.

MARY ELLEN PLEASANT
Bennett Jr., Lerone. "The Mystery of Mary Ellen Pleasant." Ebony Magazine, April 1979. Johnson Publishing Company, 1979.

EUGENE BULLARD
Haton, Claude. "First black US pilot flew for France." The Daily Mail, February 14, 2013. Hudson, New York: Columbia-Greene Media, 2016. Web. December 5, 2016. <http://www.registerstar.com/the_daily_mail/news/article_a07cf76e-7668-11e2-9020-0019bb2963f4.html>.

BELL HOOKS
"Bell Hooks: A chat with the Author of 'All About Love: New Visions.'" CNN.com, February 17, 2000. Cable News Network, 2001. Web. December 5, 2016. <http://www.cnn.com/chat/transcripts/2000/2/hooks/index.html>.